Accelerated Wisdom

Accelerated Wisdom

50 Practical Insights for Today's Superintendent

Howard C. Carlson

Published in partnership with the
American Association of School Administrators

ROWMAN & LITTLEFIELD
Lanham • Boulder • New York • London

Published by Rowman & Littlefield
An imprint of The Rowman & Littlefield Publishing Group, Inc.
4501 Forbes Boulevard, Suite 200, Lanham, Maryland 20706
www.rowman.com

6 Tinworth Street, London SE11 5AL, United Kingdom

Copyright © 2018 by Howard C. Carlson

All rights reserved. No part of this book may be reproduced in any form or by any electronic or mechanical means, including information storage and retrieval systems, without written permission from the publisher, except by a reviewer who may quote passages in a review.

British Library Cataloguing in Publication Information Available

Library of Congress Cataloging-in-Publication Data
Names: Carlson, Howard C., author.
Title: Accelerated wisdom : 50 practical insights for today's superintendent / Howard C. Carlson.
Description: Lanham, Maryland : Rowman & Littlefield, [2018] | Includes bibliographical references.
Identifiers: LCCN 2018039641 (print) | LCCN 2018050412 (ebook) | ISBN 9781475846270 (electronic) | ISBN 9781475846256 (cloth : alk. paper) | ISBN 9781475846263 (pbk. : alk. paper)
Subjects: LCSH: School superintendents—Handbooks, manuals, etc. | School management and organization—Handbooks, manuals, etc. | Educational leadership—Handbooks, manuals, etc.
Classification: LCC LB2831.7 (ebook) | LCC LB2831.7 .C37 2018 (print) | DDC 371.2/011—dc23
LC record available at https://lccn.loc.gov/2018039641

Contents

Preface	ix
Acknowledgments	xi
Chapter 1: Keeping Track	**1**
A Brief Story . . .	1
Introduction	1
Concept 1—Calendar Cards	2
Concept 2—Composition Books and Notepads	2
Concept 3—Digital Archives	3
Concept 4—E-Mail Management	4
Concept 5—Organizing Your Day	5
Concept 6—Organizational Checklists	6
Connecting the Dots in Chapter 1	9
Chapter 2: How to Navigate Requests, Concerns, Questions, and New Proposals	**11**
A Brief Story . . .	11
Introduction	12
Concept 7—Responding to Verbal Requests or Concerns	12
Concept 8—Research before Reacting	13
Concept 9—Preplan Spontaneous Responses	13
Concept 10—Generalities versus Specifics	14
Concept 11—Responding to Questions during Public Meetings	15
Concept 12—Responding to the Media	15
Concept 13—Reacting to New Proposals and Ideas	17
Concept 14—Promoting Ideas, Concepts, and Organizational Changes	17

Concept 15—The Change Continuum: Hard, Harder, Hardest … 22
Connecting the Dots in Chapter 2 … 24

Chapter 3: Hiring, Supervising, and Mentoring Employees … 25
A Brief Story … 25
Introduction … 26
Concept 16—Technical Competence versus Emotional Intelligence and Character … 26
Concept 17—Minoring in the Majors … 27
Concept 18—Circuit Training (Administrator Induction) … 28
Concept 19—Establishing New or Redefined Expectations … 30
Concept 20—Expectation Clarity and Communication for Administrators … 33
Concept 21—Superintendent/Administrative Assistant Team … 35
Concept 22—Supervisory Continuum … 37
Concept 23—Interview Questions That Reveal Core Beliefs … 39
Connecting the Dots in Chapter 3 … 39

Chapter 4: Leadership and Decision Making … 41
A Brief Story … 41
Introduction … 42
Concept 24—Decisions: I Make, I Confer, I Delegate … 42
Concept 25—Leadership Is Gray … 45
Concept 26—Tyranny of the Urgent … 45
Concept 27—Organizational Virus … 47
Concept 28—The Blunt Realities of Leadership … 47
Concept 29—Tight-Loose Leadership … 50
Concept 30—Root Cause Analysis … 50
Connecting the Dots in Chapter 4 … 52

Chapter 5: Politics, Legislative Influence, and Local Campaigns … 55
A Brief Story … 55
Introduction … 56
Concept 31—Develop a District Profile … 56
Concept 32—Getting to Know Your Legislators … 57
Concept 33—Becoming a Key Legislative Constituent … 58
Concept 34—Local Politics … 59
Concept 35—Policy versus Politics … 61
Concept 36—Levies, Bonds, and Overrides … 62
Connecting the Dots in Chapter 5 … 66

Chapter 6: Mastering School Board Relationships — **67**
A Brief Story . . . — 67
Introduction — 68
Concept 37—Meaningful Board Interaction — 68
Concept 38—Board Guidance on Handling Complaints — 71
Concept 39—The Board Operating Protocol — 72
Concept 40—Responding to Board Member Requests — 75
Concept 41—The Friday Update — 76
Concept 42—New Board Member Orientation — 79
Concept 43—Board Retreats — 81
Connecting the Dots in Chapter 6 — 82

Chapter 7: Living the Superintendency — **85**
A Brief Story . . . — 85
Introduction — 86
Concept 44—Four Scenarios — 86
Concept 45—Entry Plans — 87
Concept 46—Potholes and Pitfalls — 93
Concept 47—Superintendent Mentorship — 97
Concept 48—Life Balance and Health — 99
Concept 49—Branding Your District — 102
Concept 50—Knowing When to Leave — 104
Connecting the Dots in Chapter 7 — 106

Conclusion: Accelerated Wisdom — 109

References — 111

About the Author — 113

Preface

All leaders desire wisdom, but unfortunately it is a rare and oftentimes illusive commodity. We all strive to gain wisdom, but it normally comes through trial and error, challenge, observation, and experience. It can't be bought, but rather must be recognized when seen, heard, or imparted.

As leaders we spend our careers sifting through mounds of articles and Internet posts, reading books, attending scores of conferences, and talking to numerous individuals in search of wisdom that will make us more successful. We engage in an ongoing journey to enhance our knowledge because everyone knows that a wise leader is an effective leader.

In the seminal leadership book, *The First 90 Days: Critical Success Strategies for New Leaders at All Levels*, Michael Watkins (2003) seeks to help individuals who are experiencing a leadership transition. Watkins points to fundamental principles which hasten the transition to leadership success, not only for new leaders but also for anyone making a shift. The wisdom he imparts to the reader, gained through his own observation, research, and experience is profound.

The goal of this book is similar but a bit more expansive. My hope is to provide superintendents, regardless of tenure, with a set of tested and proven concepts that accelerate wisdom (and ultimately success) in their day-to-day leadership.

The concepts that follow, although not meant to be all-encompassing, provide thoughts and ideas that can accelerate leadership success. The concepts are standalone in nature, and thus you can read the book cover to cover or just flip to Concept 20 and jump around based on your particular needs and interests.

Each concept is intended to provide leaders with a shorter path to effectiveness and success. Some of the concepts will likely be ideas that you already practice, others may produce an aha moment, but all are tested by time and experience.

I hope you enjoy this book and the individual concepts outlined in the chapters to come. I also hope that you will be willing to share with me the nuggets of wisdom that have worked in your experience (my email is hcarlsonthesupt@gmail.com). Leadership wisdom is not a finite commodity, but rather something from which we can all benefit.

Okay, let's get started!

Acknowledgments

I wish to acknowledge the contribution of the following reviewers and editors for their time, effort, and assistance.

- Mark Joraanstad, PhD, executive director, Arizona School Administrators, Phoenix, Arizona
- Andrew Wannemacher, superintendent, Aguila Elementary School District, Aguila, Arizona
- Andrew Carlson, student, Arizona State University, Tempe, Arizona
- BreeAnna Carlson, student, Arizona State University, Tempe, Arizona
- Arthur Pulis, business consultant, Wickenburg, Arizona
- James Watt, former Secretary of the Interior under President Reagan, Wickenburg, Arizona
- Kevin Chase, superintendent, ESD 105, Yakima, Washington
- Theresa West, EdD, leadership coach and consultant, Falls Church, Virginia

Chapter 1

Keeping Track

A BRIEF STORY...

Ron, a seasoned superintendent with fifteen years of experience, enjoyed interacting with people and considered himself knowledgeable regarding the change process. The district he served, which was in a suburban area with over 20,000 students, was growing, and thus lots of changes were occurring. Attending multiple meetings on a daily basis was quite common for Ron, and he enjoyed interacting with people so much that he often trusted his memory to retain key facts and tasks to be completed.

One day, Ron received a letter from a foundation that was funding a teacher development project in the district indicating that due to the fact that a funding renewal request had not been submitted the project would conclude at the end of the school year. Ron was devastated, and when he contacted the foundation, he was reminded that the renewal request was discussed with him eight months ago during a meeting. The problem was that on that day Ron had been in six back-to-back meetings and failed to record this important detail.

After experiencing the loss of this major funding source in his district Ron committed to using both calendar cards and composition books to record important details from conversations and meetings. It was a tough lesson to learn, but it changed the way Ron operated in the superintendency from that day forward.

INTRODUCTION

Organizing the mass of information superintendents are confronted with on a daily basis can be daunting. Although methods of organization can vary and should be driven by what works for each individual, the goal of this chapter is to outline the types of information district leaders encounter and provide some practical techniques for capturing important thoughts and ideas.

Superintendents routinely confront the need to remember multiple issues by day's end or to recall information from months past. If they do not have an effective way to keep track of this information, they are likely to drop the ball, which can negatively impact their credibility thus harming their leadership potential.

CONCEPT 1—CALENDAR CARDS

An effective way for superintendents to keep track of their day and to record important notes for future action is through the use of calendar cards. Superintendents can ask their administrative assistant to print them a business-sized card using their calendar program, which shows the schedule for that day and the various activities that must be completed. (Many individuals use Microsoft Outlook, but this process could be completed in Google or any system.)

The calendar card can then be placed in the superintendent's purse, shirt pocket, or phone case allowing for quick reference and making the card available for taking notes. Of course, superintendents can always check their schedule on their phone, but the calendar card enables individuals to take a quick note while effectively interacting with others.

On almost a daily basis, through a conversation or sitting in a meeting, superintendents will find occasion to record an item on the calendar card. All too often administrators don't take the time to make quick notes or record tasks to be completed, believing they will remember to record the items later. In many cases the busyness of their day takes precedence and important items are forgotten.

Although this is a simple method, it works. It will assist you in staying organized, which is important for your professional reputation.

CONCEPT 2—COMPOSITION BOOKS AND NOTEPADS

It is amazing how often superintendents are required to recall details from meetings or important conversations months or even years later. As such we archive our e-mails into folders, but we also need methods to record important information from meetings or conversations on a daily basis. As many of these situations require active listening and at times interpersonal communication, we must record important points while remaining personally engaged.

Superintendents can address this dilemma in a variety of ways such as capturing notes on a computer during the interaction, waiting until the conclusion of the event to record information from memory, or taking handwritten notes as the discussion proceeds. All three methods can work, but many prefer to keep a composition book or notepad to record key notes and information during the dialogue.

The composition book and notepad options are often preferred because it is easier to interact genuinely while at the same time recording crucial information. Writing a few notes by hand during these situations tends to be less distracting and gives superintendents a reference point if they desire to record more information later. It also provides a set of items that can organize key tasks to be accomplished. One colleague, Dan Parris, numbers his notes so that he can refer to them later as they are being completed. As an example, he can give his notes to his team and later ask whether item #26 is finished yet. Dan indicates that by taking notes you validate the conversation, achieve the ability to prioritize your work, and gain the satisfaction of completing a task once crossed off the list.

A seasoned superintendent's shelf will often contain a number of composition books and notepads that have been filled up with information over the years. Most find that they are required to go back to these books and notepads frequently to review information from a meeting or conversation that took place months or years back.

Superintendents find these methods of organization to be especially important when they are asked to recall personnel interactions or decisions. Administrators engage in important conversations on a regular basis, and when required to recall the event at a later date their memory can fail them because they did not take action to record key details.

Superintendents who make a habit out of recording daily conversations, interactions, and meetings will enhance their effectiveness and credibility when questions related to past events arise. Although it may seem easier (or less of a hassle) to rely upon our memories in the midst of overloaded daily schedules, in the end this strategy is doomed to fail. The key concept here is that we must develop and follow some method for capturing, recording, preserving, and organizing important information on a daily basis to be successful in the superintendency.

CONCEPT 3—DIGITAL ARCHIVES

One of the challenges superintendents have with organizing and maintaining important information is that it can come in various forms. In other words, one might attend a negotiations meeting and need to gather information from a white board, several documents, and handwritten notes in a composition book or on a notepad.

Clearly it is important to retain all of this information, but district leaders must make decisions regarding how to do so. One can maintain each of these items in their original form and at different locations, but a better alternative might be to archive all three mediums in a single digital format.

Digital archiving can take a bit of time, but it is extremely powerful. Not only do superintendents record the information forever, but they do so in a manner where one can access it from any location where an Internet connection is available. In the preceding example of the negotiations meeting superintendents could store all of their information in a digital negotiations folder.

To do so one could take a picture of the whiteboard contents on one's smartphone and upload it to the digital folder. In addition, documents that were handed out could be scanned and uploaded too. Finally, superintendents could take a picture of their handwritten notes in a composition book and upload them to the digital folder so that all mediums of information from the meeting would be saved in one location and available for future use.

Clearly it can take some time to pull together all of the information that might be available in a single meeting, but for a leader's most important tasks it is a great way to record the material. There are many programs and tools available that allow superintendents to do this. A few of the most commonly used, some of which are free, include:

- Evernote
- Simplenote
- Google Keep
- Microsoft OneNote
- Google Docs
- Rocketbooks

CONCEPT 4—E-MAIL MANAGEMENT

Managing e-mail can be a daunting task for superintendents considering many of them receive in excess of 100 messages per day. Often, a number of the e-mails are advertisements, blog post notifications, daily education news updates, or other information that can be quickly reviewed and deleted. The real challenge comes in determining which e-mails to keep, which to delete, and how the important messages can be maintained for future reference.

Superintendents tend to use two primary types of e-mail management systems today, Microsoft Outlook or Internet-based systems such as Google's Gmail. In addition, superintendents are normally connected to e-mail through their desktop computer, smartphone, laptop, iPad, and at times using remote devices. The bottom line is that all connections must work seamlessly so the superintendent can retrieve and send messages from multiple locations on demand.

So, let's discuss the choice to delete or maintain e-mail for future reference. First, seasoned superintendents will likely agree that rather than deleting any e-mail it is best to either archive all messages or let deleted messages grow without limit in the system. The reason for this approach, as mentioned in previous sections, is that superintendents never know when they will need a deleted e-mail from a previous period.

All too often a personnel issue, legal issue, or public records request will generate the need to search previous e-mail messages for vital information. Of course, the district's IT personnel may not appreciate the size of the superintendent's deleted e-mail folder, but for the district's leader, records must be preserved for future reference.

Second, superintendents need a robust folder and subfolder organization system if Outlook or Google labels are preferred. The main idea here is that the volume of e-mail received must be organized in such a manner as to be easily accessible and searchable.

Some superintendents organize their e-mail by school district department and school, while others organize by topic (e.g., board, discipline, legislature, parents) or using professional administrator standards. Regardless, superintendents must find an organization system that best fits their personality, style, and thinking pattern so they can easily search for and retrieve e-mail when needed.

CONCEPT 5—ORGANIZING YOUR DAY

One hallmark of an effective superintendent is how the individual organizes his or her day. Most of us simply follow what is listed on our schedule, but there are ways to operate in a more efficient and organized manner.

After attending a recent leadership conference, a colleague, Debbie Hodgkiss, introduced our cabinet team to a presentation made by David Allen of vitalsmarts.com on this topic. The presentation was based on David Allen's book titled *Getting Things Done: The Art of Stress-Free Productivity* (2015).

In the presentation, Mr. Allen outlined what he calls *core tips* related to becoming more organized and effective. Although his complete system is very comprehensive, let's focus on what he says about a leader's daily calendar.

Mr. Allen describes one's daily calendar as *fixed and certain* but points out that it lacks organized action. In other words, a leader's daily calendar likely provides a list of tasks to be completed during the day (e.g., projects to complete, meetings to attend, and decisions to consider), but it requires further clarity to become actionable. To make this transition, Allen explains that leaders need a *next actions list* prior to starting the day, which in essence breaks their calendar tasks down into purposeful activities.

To clarify how to proceed with each calendar task, leaders need to ask three questions:

- Is there an action to be completed?
- What is the next action?
- Who should complete the action?

Clearly, based on the ever-changing needs in a superintendent's daily schedule, both the calendar and next action list (which can be tracked in systems such as Google Tasks) will need to be revised each morning (or the night before). One needs to block out time each day for both reflecting on one's calendar and revising the list. Once we get into this pattern we need to begin rebalancing our list each week so that ongoing actions don't fall off our plate.

To be honest calendar organization and action planning is difficult and often will be the last thing superintendents want to worry about each day. District leaders often fall prey to the *tyranny of the urgent*, and without a method to keep organized they either end up addressing tasks in an ineffective manner or the tasks are forgotten until someone brings them up again.

The system outlined here is but one organizational concept, and although it will keep superintendents working efficiently they may have another method that works better for them personally. Regardless, as district leaders with challenging schedules, we must conform to some system of organization to be seen as effective by our staff, the board, and the public.

CONCEPT 6—ORGANIZATIONAL CHECKLISTS

School districts have a multitude of reports to submit, tasks to manage, and laws to comply with throughout the year. How do superintendents and their cabinet members keep track of what must be accomplished and ensure items do not slip off the plate?

A method many cabinet members and superintendents use is an *organizational efficiency checklist*. (Exhibit 6.1 shows an example of a checklist, covering ongoing items and one month of the fiscal year.) It is a living document and is updated regularly based on changes from the state, or to add other tasks that must be managed frequently.

Exhibit 6.1 Organizational Efficiency Checklist

General/Ongoing

Location	Due	Item
Business office	Report immediately	Employee injury report
Business office	Report immediately	Equipment loss/theft
Business office	Report within 8 hours	Student injury report (within 8 hours of discovery)
Business office	Two weeks lead time	Requisition student activity
Business office	Prior to working	Overtime request
Business office	Due 1 week after travel	Travel reimbursement claims
Business office	Immediately	Transfer/disposal of fixed assets
Business office	First Friday in June	All POs to close
District office	Immediately	Mandatory reporting of suspected child abuse to peace officer by phone or person
District office	Within 72 hour of oral report	Written report of suspected child abuse to peace officer
Federal programs	Within 30 days of registration	Parental notification and consent forms—new ELL students
Federal projects	Ongoing	Update new hires into HQT input system
Governing board	Third Thursday of the month	Regular governing board meeting (6 p.m.)
Governing board	Ongoing	Board adoption of supplementary materials (Occurs 60 days after materials are put on display.)
Student services	Immediately	Mandatory reporting of suspected child abuse to peace officer by phone or person
Payroll	Every Monday	Timecards due in payroll (If Monday is a holiday, time cards due Tuesday.)
School site	Ongoing	Referral, suspension data entered into Power School
School site	Four time/year	Lock-down drill
School site	State monitoring may occur any time	All original appropriately certified documentation remains at school site in secure location for state
School site	Once per month	Fire drill
Superintendent	First Wednesday of the month	Curriculum staff meeting (12:00)
Superintendent	Second and fourth Tuesday of the month	Admin. meeting (1:30 p.m.–3:30 p.m.)
Superintendent	Fourth Wednesday of the Month	Operations meeting

(Continued)

Exhibit 6.1 (Continued)

July

Location	Due	Item
Student services—Galileo	July	Prep for beginning of the year benchmarks
District office	7/1	Free and reduced lunch letters out
Student services	7/7	Order AZELLA materials
Director of business services	7/15	Budget adoption
Superintendent	7/15	Create school opening/activities calendar for beginning of school year
Superintendent	7/19	Back to school letter—new teachers/returning teachers
Superintendent	7/19	Back to school letter—classified staff
Superintendent	7/21–22	Admin. retreat
Administrators	7/22	Back-to-school articles—submit to superintendent
Superintendent's secretary	7/23	Invite school board to new teacher lunch and opening day
Superintendent	7/26	Back-to-school articles to newspaper
School site	7/26	High school—senior orientation
School site	7/27	High school—junior orientation
School site	7/28	High school—sophomore orientation
School site	7/29	High school—freshman orientation
School site	7/30	High school—makeup day
Student services	7/30	Provide data from Power School to Galileo to load (this operation takes Galileo 7 days)
Student services—AzMERIT	7/31	Update AzMERIT in Power School /AzMERIT 3-year graphs/ AzMERIT rank order by grade level

Cabinet members and superintendents should reserve a portion of their weekly agenda to review the checklist and to make sure necessary components are being addressed. As discussed in Concept 4 the team also determines whether action is required, who will complete that action, upon what timeline, and how the action will be communicated.

CONNECTING THE DOTS IN CHAPTER 1

Effectively staying on top of the many tasks that superintendents must individually complete and efficiently leading the organization are of paramount importance to their success as the district's leader. The superintendency is simply too complex and fast moving to not have a solid plan for *keeping track*.

Although everyone has preferences when it comes to managing his or her daily and organizational activities, the key is to have a solid operational system in place. Hopefully the information outlined in this chapter provided opportunity for thought, reflection, and conversation regarding these important issues.

Chapter 2

How to Navigate Requests, Concerns, Questions, and New Proposals

A BRIEF STORY...

In the early months of Colleen's superintendency, a position she entered after years as a high school principal, she was frequently approached by the staff and community regarding changes to be made in the district or new ideas to consider.

Colleen would diligently listen to each plea and was careful to indicate that she would take the proposed change or new idea under consideration. It did not take long for Colleen to realize that she was receiving so many requests that it was becoming hard to remember the details of each item.

At this point, through conversation with a neighboring superintendent, Colleen learned that it can be helpful to ask those proposing a change or new idea to provide her a written proposal. Implementing this concept reduced Colleen's stress level tenfold. Rather than taking on the responsibility of remembering the details of each request, which she truly wanted to hear, Colleen could now put that responsibility back on the person bringing the proposal forward.

Interestingly, Colleen learned that when she used this approach not everyone followed through and thus the number of proposals decreased significantly. It became apparent that some people wanted to dump an issue on Colleen, but did not want to put the time in to truly address the subject.

Colleen learned a valuable lesson through the wisdom of her neighboring superintendent and from that point forward she always passed this technique on to new superintendents whom she mentored.

INTRODUCTION

Superintendents are faced with requests, concerns, and questions on almost a daily basis. While these items may come during formal meetings, often they arise through spur of the moment interactions. Superintendents may be at a school, a community or social event, or even at the grocery store. At these moments members of the public or district staff are focused on their issue or concern, and superintendents are faced with how to respond.

In addition (although on a less frequent basis) superintendents are required to engage with the media, promote organizational changes, and react to new proposals. The question is this: What practical insights can be gleaned to give superintendents a framework to most effectively handle these situations?

The aim of this chapter is to help district leaders think through these scenarios and to provide tools that can be of assistance. Superintendents who enter these circumstances prepared and confident will have a much greater chance of achieving successful outcomes.

CONCEPT 7—RESPONDING TO VERBAL REQUESTS OR CONCERNS

As stated earlier, superintendents are frequently approached with requests or concerns that can run on a continuum from information about the district posed by a member of the public to more complex matters such as personnel issues. Superintendents want to be helpful and be seen in a good light from a public relations (PR) perspective, but they must have a strategy to handle verbal requests and concerns so they don't become inundated and fail to respond in an appropriate or effective manner.

If the request is very simple and quick to record, superintendents can use their calendar card (Concept 1) to make a short note and then move on to their next activity. Alternatively, if the request is lengthy or includes important details, it is best to ask the person to send an e-mail or text regarding the item.

The request will have been heard, but superintendents gain time to research the issue prior to responding. Notice that an e-mail or text was suggested, not a phone call. The goal is to get the request or concern in writing. A phone conversation relies upon the person receiving the message to remember what was stated, which at times can be left up to interpretation, or in the worst-case scenario the story can change down the road. The written word is memorialized, so as superintendents take action or are required recall the situation, it is much easier to achieve clarity regarding the message that was conveyed.

CONCEPT 8—RESEARCH BEFORE REACTING

On numerous occasions throughout our careers we have watched administrators and other leaders react without understanding the facts or the full scope of the situation (many of us are guilty too!). Unfortunately, this issue is not limited to rookie administrators but at times seasoned professionals as well. It also is prevalent among individuals one will encounter on a daily basis in the superintendency such as board members, parents, community members, and elected officials.

When faced with situations that stir our emotions we need to have the metacognitive skills to stop and reflect before reacting. Of course, this is not always easy, but rather than assuming the worst, superintendents need to step back and consider that possibly there is an alternative explanation.

Clearly this is not just a work skill, but one that impacts us in our broader life too. The key is to train ourselves to ask questions before proceeding toward making a statement or decision. Obviously, this takes time and reflection, and thus a better process in these situations is stop, analyze possible explanations or alternatives, research these options, and then once comfortable, react or make a decision.

Superintendents who have time and are not faced with the need for a quick reaction or decision can consider the *root cause analysis* process (Barsalou, 2015) to better analyze what might have transpired in a particular circumstance. Root cause analysis (Concept 28) and its various problem-solving tools (i.e., the *5 whys*) are a method designed to help individuals distill problems down to their fundamental source. Using a process like root cause analysis forces us to reflect and to question the reason for problems and this in turn produces more appropriate reactions and ultimately more effective decisions.

CONCEPT 9—PREPLAN SPONTANEOUS RESPONSES

The preplanned spontaneous responses concept was shared by a friend and neighbor, Jim Watt, who served in President Reagan's Cabinet as the secretary of the Interior. Jim has functioned at the highest levels of leadership, and he pointed out recently that administrators often go into board meetings or other events anticipating that certain questions will be posed.

Of course, superintendents will not necessarily know exactly how the question will be stated, but they can make solid assumptions. If district leaders think these issues through prior to meetings or events, they can reflect upon what will be said on the topic and ultimately provide a more informed, accurate, and concise response.

Clearly, many leaders do this intuitively but have never particularly thought about it in this manner. Others may not have considered this option but can benefit from preparing for issues and challenges in this way. Although simple, the concept of preplanning spontaneous responses gives leaders the ability to answer questions that will likely arise.

Oftentimes, simple, yet profound, concepts like this are important in displaying wisdom that enables us to achieve and maintain success in the superintendency. As with other communication processes, being prepared with examples or turns of phrase can increase our credibility with the board and our constituents.

CONCEPT 10—GENERALITIES VERSUS SPECIFICS

Oftentimes when a staff member, community resident, or parent presents a problem, they describe it as an issue of general concern. As an example, the issue is commonly stated as follows: "The teachers are upset because they did not receive their bonus checks prior to the beginning of the school year"; or "the parents don't like the new math curriculum."

Of course, it is possible *all* of the teachers may be upset about the bonus checks or that *all* of the parents may not like the math curriculum, but more often than not, concerns are stated in general terms in an effort to raise the superintendent's level of anxiety in hopes that it will prompt quick action.

The question is, how should superintendents react in situations where generalized concerns are raised? The first step is to unpack the issue with the person lodging the complaint by asking specific questions. The superintendent's goals are to determine how widespread the issue might be and how urgent the matter is at this point in time. Typically asking specific questions provides one with enough information to determine how to proceed.

Because generalized statements are often meant to illicit a reaction, superintendents must guard against replying without complete information and potentially being manipulated by the individual raising the concern. It may be that only a small group of teachers are upset about not receiving their bonus checks, and the superintendent's reaction in this situation will be much different from how it would be if indeed the majority of teachers have a concern.

To the extent superintendents can gain specifics related to a concern, determining how widespread and urgent the issue is at this stage gives them the ability to formulate a thoughtful, prudent response. The person's goal by using generalizations, as stated earlier, is to make the issue both bigger and more critical. Superintendents must not get caught in this trap, but rather ascertain through a series of questions, the size of the issue, and its level of importance.

CONCEPT 11—RESPONDING TO QUESTIONS DURING PUBLIC MEETINGS

Superintendents oftentimes find themselves in public forums ranging from board meetings to presentations to town hall events. As part of these events, superintendents can be asked questions by board members or members of the public, and their response can have important consequences.

In these situations we are focused on multiple issues simultaneously, such as searching at a mental level for the answer and paying attention to our poise and the quality of our spoken response. As this is the case, we must be very careful how we react in the public forum.

One of the best ways to handle situations where we don't directly know the answer off the top of our head (or have a preplanned spontaneous response) is to simply state "let me get back to you on that." If pressed, one can further indicate "I want to research the question so that I can provide an accurate response."

Most individuals will respect this approach, and superintendents can then respond to the individual when emotional levels have subsided and the leader has had time to reflect upon their response. In some cases individuals will continue to press us in the public forum because emotions are running high and they desire a public debate.

If you stick to the script outlined earlier, which is both reasonable and respectful, district leaders will most often find that it defuses the issue and creates an opportunity for a constructive response at a later point in time.

CONCEPT 12—RESPONDING TO THE MEDIA

One of the more stressful aspects of the superintendency can be responding to the media, especially if the situation is borne out of a negative or tragic situation. Oftentimes the problem is the superintendent won't know exactly what he or she will be asked and therefore it is prudent to have a previously planned response going into the conversation. Depending upon the scenario the superintendent may read from a prepared media release. If the interview will include questions from the media, district leaders should be prepared with certain key messages that they plan to convey regardless of the questions asked.

Much has been written on this topic, and through further research one can expand his or her expertise, but the goal of this section is to provide a few rudimentary, proven tools for superintendents' use when faced with a media interview.

As stated earlier, it is imperative to have a planned response prior to going into a media interview. Superintendents who do so without any form of preparation will undoubtedly find that it does not go well. So, what are some basic techniques that superintendents can use? Next, one will find a simple process to follow, regardless of whether the interview is with a print, online, or television outlet.

Media Interview Process

1. *Know the reason for the interview.* The first step in the process is to understand the reason for the interview. If the reporter is not clear, be sure to gain clarification prior to agreeing to be interviewed. Remember: You are in charge in this situation and if the reporter is going to gain your perspective, he or she must be clear, honest, and forthright about what the topic of discussion might be focused upon.
2. *Create reflection time before responding.* Never respond to a member of the media without knowing the reason for the interview and taking the time to reflect (following the response template outlined later in #4 of this list). If you happen to be caught off guard by the media showing up at your office or receive an unplanned phone call, indicate that you can meet with the individual or call him or her at a different time. Even if you provide yourself an hour to prepare, you always want time to work through the response template prior to an interview.
3. *Determine whether to conduct the interview.* Is the reporter looking for a comment regarding a controversial land development project near a school site? If so, it may be that you don't want to wade into the fray. Alternatively, if it is about a fight at one of your high schools to not respond will send the message that the district is trying to hide important information. The key here is that you don't need to answer all enquiries, but you must think through each situation individually regarding how it impacts the district and your responsibility to respond as its representative.
4. *Response template.*

    a. Identify two to three points you want to communicate regarding the situation or incident and prepare a written media release if appropriate.
    b. Reflect upon the questions you might be asked and how you can use a *communication bridge* (Meisburg, 2014) to return the conversation to your two or three key points on each occasion. A communication bridge is where you attempt to drive the conversation back to the points you wish to discuss. As an example, you might use phrases such as: "You make a good point, but here is our concern," or "I understand the concern, although . . .", or "I am not sure about that, but I can tell you. . . ."

As stated at the beginning of this concept, interacting with the media can be a stressful endeavor, and there are many strategies that one can glean from organizations such as the National School Public Relations Association (NSPRA) or The School Superintendents Association (AASA) to strengthen their skill set.

The information outlined in this section provides superintendents with the basics from which to operate when faced with a media inquiry. It is recommended that superintendents keep the template close by so that it is easily accessible when needed. The challenge is that media interactions don't often come on a predictable basis, so one must always be prepared to outline their thoughts prior to taking the phone call or stepping outside to complete a television interview.

CONCEPT 13—REACTING TO NEW PROPOSALS AND IDEAS

On multiple occasions throughout one's career as superintendent, one will be approached with new ideas from staff, administrators, board members, and the public. After careful thought, reflection and planning a new idea might be helpful to implement, but alternatively it may not be feasible or in some situations might be manipulative in nature.

Individuals are excited and typically motivated regarding their new idea and hope that their superintendent will be too. Some ideas may be truly innovative, but others may be unrealistic or even self-serving.

So how do superintendents respond when being pitched a new idea? As the district's leader it is important to listen and validate the person's enthusiasm, but the leader must also create time for reflection and a thoughtful, researched response. One of the best ways to respond when someone promotes a new idea is to ask for a *written proposal* (like Colleen did at the beginning of the chapter). Using this approach superintendents can achieve clarity in terms of what the person is proposing and also gain valuable time to research and reflect upon the idea prior to providing a decision.

Although in the end the promoter of the new idea may not be happy with the final decision, district leaders can show they listened, reflected upon the issue, and provided a thoughtful response. Superintendents, who follow this process, rather than reacting immediately, will be viewed by those whom they serve as attentive to constituents' ideas and diligent in their decision-making processes.

CONCEPT 14—PROMOTING IDEAS, CONCEPTS, AND ORGANIZATIONAL CHANGES

Superintendents are frequently faced with the need to *sell* an idea, change, or concept. To move the organization forward and to successfully implement the goals that have been established, the superintendent must convince others that the changes being proposed will be fruitful.

The question is, how to do this successfully? In the paragraphs that follow methods are identified that have proven successful and will assist superintendents in doing this heavy lifting as they seek to move their districts to the next academic and operational level.

In *Changing Minds: The Art and Science of Changing Our Own and Other People's Minds*, author Howard Gardner (2006) identifies seven techniques that can be used to promote acceptance of an idea or encourage change of thought related to a concept. Gardner refers to these techniques as *levers*, which can help individuals understand and accept new ideas, concepts, or changes.

To dig deeper into these seven levers, one should read Gardner's *Changing Minds* book (or *So Now You're the Superintendent*, a book I coauthored with Dr. John Eller). In the *So Now You're the Superintendent* book, the seven levers are more fully discussed in the context of the superintendency.

To begin, let's briefly review a list of Gardner's seven levers:

- Reason
  - The idea of providing the pros related to a new concept and addressing any cons that might exist.
- Research
  - Tying the concept back to research, data, or best practice.
- Resonance
  - Tapping into arguments for the change that "make sense" to people.
- Representational redescriptions
  - Presenting the message in a variety of formats (i.e., stories, graphical representations, written materials).
- Resources and rewards
  - Using resources and rewards to support individuals who adopt the new concept as an incentive to achieve *buy-in* and acceptance.
- Real-world events
  - Using national, state, or local events to effect an idea, change, or concept (i.e., discussing a school shooting somewhere in the country to create urgency related to updating local school crisis management plans).

- Resistances
  - Taking time to reflect individually, or with your team, regarding potential points of resistance to an idea, concept, or change.

Over the years superintendents will likely find use for each of the levers at varying points in time. In fact, it can often be fruitful to use multiple levers simultaneously.

As an example when one district was attempting to shift to a web-based curriculum management system (CMS) it was determined a primary *resistance* to implementation was that teachers had antiquated computers on their desks and this prevented optimal use of the CMS.

In response, the district used the concept of *resources and rewards* to provide new computers in recognition of teachers' work to use the system on a daily basis. By combining the two levers simultaneously the district was able to successfully navigate the change and move forward toward success.

The levers listed provide a helpful framework upon which to build the promotion of the district's idea, concept, or change, but there is a second component that must be included if superintendents are to be successful. That component is *emotion*.

If the idea, concept, or change does not engage people at an emotional level, it will not have the necessary impact to be successful. It is often said that *a picture is worth a thousand words*, and the reason this is true is because an image touches people on an emotional level.

If one reflects upon this concept, one will find examples in one's own life, as all of us can. In *Teaching That Sticks*, an article written by authors Heath and Dan Heath, they explain, "That's what emotion does for an idea—it makes people care. It makes people feel something" (2010, p. 8).

So how do superintendents infuse emotion into the promotion of their ideas, concepts, or change processes? The methods are not particularly hard to identify:

- Using pictures, sounds, movie clips
- Telling a story
- Providing a physical example
- Displaying a chart
- Using simulations
- Using slogans, catch-phrases, or general names to describe the change
- Role-playing and so forth

Our challenge lies in how we connect our idea with an appropriate emotional response from those whom we wish to impact.

As an example, if we are proposing a curriculum change to close the achievement gap between groups of students in our district, we might begin the process by depicting the gap graphically (*research*), but also ask an individual from the community representing the identified student group to come in and tell a story about how children in his or her community live (*emotion*).

In addition, the speaker might highlight how significantly going to college can impact not only individual students but also their entire family (*emotion*). In this example we used one of Gardner's levers to promote the idea but also added the emotional component of storytelling. Combined, this two-step method of promoting ideas, concepts, or changes can be very powerful.

One final component to discuss in this section relates to *timing*. Superintendents may have thought it confounding at times during their career how an idea, concept, or change, which seemed important to the school or organization, would fail to take hold even though leaders believed it was approached in an appropriate manner.

At that point in one's career one may not have fully understood how important timing was to the success of an initiative. Of course, many of us have likely since learned that although it may be the right thing to do, it may not be the right time to do it.

Timing makes the change process tricky and highly unpredictable. Although we can use Gardner's levers to promote understanding and develop approaches that stimulate an emotional connection, if the idea, concept, or change comes at the wrong time it will fail.

Ultimately, there is no way to predict with certainty the correct timing for an initiative. One must study the culture and context of the school district, looking at various aspects of the organization, its operation and constituents, to determine if it is ready for change. (See Exhibit 14.1)

For change to occur and to be sustained, superintendents must have insight into what the culture values, how it operates, and how its formal and informal leadership views the initiative. One way to assess this piece would be to use the Windowpane Model for Analyzing Constituent Perspectives (see Exhibit 14.2).

The Windowpane Model (Eller and Carlson, 2009) enables superintendents to reflect individually or with their team regarding how groups might view the initiative. Taking the time for this reflective activity can enable superintendents (and their teams) to more effectively gauge the timing and marketing for an initiative.

Although as stated earlier one cannot *time* an initiative, it is possible to mitigate some of the uncertainty through using tools like the Culture and Change Template and the Window Pane Model for Analyzing Constituent Perspectives.

Exhibit 14.1 Culture and Change Template

The following is a sample Culture and Change Template. It may not work in all situations, but it does provide a general outline regarding how to effectively initiate a change process. A precursor to the change process is to develop relationships with those who will be expected to implement the change. It is also important to always study the reasons for the existing process (cultural norms) prior to moving forward. Superintendents will want to convey that they will seek out the staff's thoughts and then communicate with them throughout the process.

Template Steps

- Once an item is identified for potential change, take time to understand why the process/task/procedure is currently in place. This is the "culture awareness" step. It was likely put in place for a reason, and prior to considering a change you need to know why it is done that way and who may be a champion of the current process/task/procedure. Understanding the *why* question will help you design a more successful change process.
- Speak to trusted staff members to send up a *trial balloon* regarding the potential change. Be sure to gather their feedback on how the change might be successfully implemented.
- Once you gather initial feedback, it is important to make necessary adjustments that will enhance the chances for success.
- The next step is to identify those who might help promote the change— your *champions* or *guiding coalition* (Kotter, 2012). In other words if individuals, through engagement and active participation, can *own* and present the change concept, then it is not solely an administrative initiative but rather a collaborative process.
- The next step in the process is engaging your champions or guiding coalition in presenting the *change idea* to the entire staff (or other groups). The goal is to focus on this concept as a potential way to address an issue that is being faced by the school or organization.
- At this point, if all has gone well, communicate to all involved that the change process will be pursued and additional feedback would be appreciated.
- Consider any feedback received. Some feedback will be relevant, while other feedback will be a method to protect the status quo. Remember this is the point where your champions can then stand with you to continue moving forward.
- Adjustments are made as time progresses because, as we know, change is messy and will take a period of time to sustainably implement.

Exhibit 14.2 Windowpane Model Analysis of Shifting to a New K–8 Math Curriculum (example)

Teachers' View: Need proper training and time to implement without being held immediately accountable	Principals' View: A new curriculum will enable us to increase proficiency and test scores	Parents' View: Why do we need a new curriculum? How will I help my child?
Community Members' View: How much will a new curriculum cost?	Superintendent's View: What does the research and data say about this new curriculum?	Students' View: We don't understand how this new math works. Why do we need to change?
Instructional Aides' View: How will the new curriculum impact our jobs?	Board Members' View: What do parents' think? Will it raise test scores? What is the cost?	High School Staff View: How does this curriculum align with ours? Will students come prepared?

Windowpane Model for Analyzing Constituent Perspectives Blank Template

View 1	View 2	View 3
View 4	View 5	View 6
View 7	View 8	View 9

Copyright © 2009 by Corwin Press. All rights reserved. Reprinted with permission from *So Now You're the Superintendent!* by John Eller and Howard C. Carlson. Thousand Oaks, CA: Corwin Press, www.corwinpress.com.

CONCEPT 15—THE CHANGE CONTINUUM: HARD, HARDER, HARDEST

In Concept 14, we reviewed planning for change, but that is just the beginning of the change process. Superintendents must also think through implementation and how to make change sustainable. It can be helpful to think about change on a continuum from being *hard* on the planning end of the spectrum to *hardest* when attempting to achieve sustainability.

Superintendents often see the change process as including planning and implementation, but rarely do they recognize the importance of sustainability. If district leaders don't establish a sustainable process, then all of their work will be for naught because the change they planned for and implemented will not become a permanent part of the organizational culture.

Hard

Planning for change is *hard*. It requires using *levers* (see Concept 14) to promote acceptance, along with engaging people at an emotional level. Superintendents must spend time studying those who will be impacted by the change and employ tools to assess whether the timing is right to move forward.

The more time superintendents spend planning, discussing, and reflecting upon the change process, the greater chance they will be successful. Typically, leaders get one shot at implementing a change initiative, and thus diligence and hard work in the planning process are critical.

Harder

Implementing the change process is *harder*. In other words planning is hard, but the finesse required to navigate the implementation process is even more difficult. Change is never linear; it is a process of taking one step forward and two steps back, making adjustments and modifications, spending time working through *implementation dips* (Fullan, 2004), and looking for small wins and milestones throughout the journey. Pilot projects can provide the opportunity to *test* an idea, but the fact remains that adjustments will always be required.

So to be successful, superintendents must be ready to alter their plans, understanding that reaching the goal may not follow the path initially conceived. Leaders who go into the implementation process understanding these realities guard themselves against frustration and thus begin to embrace the tweaks and adjustments as progress toward the goal to be achieved.

Hardest

Sustaining change is the *hardest*. A change that is sustained has become a part of the organizational culture and, therefore, will likely not go away unless tremendous effort is spent to modify its impact.

The only way to achieve sustainable change is to successfully focus upon and promote the planning and implementation processes and to gain *buy-in* from those in the organization. As stated earlier, sustainability is the hardest part of the change process and will be elusive if acceptance can't be achieved.

The tools discussed in Concept 14 can assist with the acceptance process, but sustained change requires ongoing maintenance. Superintendents need to remember that any time change is implemented it will have detractors, and those individuals will likely work to undermine the transformation over time if the district leader is not attentive to this reality.

Thus, it is important to continually revisit the reasons the change was implemented and why it was important for the organization. An effort to keep the impetus behind the change fresh in the minds of our constituents reduces the chance that an effort will be pursued to overturn what has been established.

CONNECTING THE DOTS IN CHAPTER 2

A lot of territory was covered in this chapter as we discussed how to navigate requests, concerns, questions, and new proposals, but many of these ideas tie together and cut across various scenarios that superintendents face.

We don't often think about concepts such as how to react to verbal requests, generalities versus specifics, responding to the media, or preparing preplanned spontaneous answers, but these ideas can help us become wiser and more thoughtful in our positions. Superintendents normally do reflect deeply regarding the promotion ideas or addressing organizational change, but with the plethora of information available the guidance can be overwhelming.

An attempt was made in this section of the chapter to tie together research and practical wisdom, which, when used in combination, can create positive outcomes. As an example, the use of Howard Gardner's *Levers of Change* coupled with the writings of Chip and Dan Heath related to engaging emotions in the change process can be very powerful.

The goal was to use the concepts outlined in this chapter to narrow the field of information required for superintendents to review on these topics, but also provide an opportunity for deep thought and reflection especially as it relates to the superintendent's specific context.

We often consider *synthesis* as the highest level of learning. To synthesize a connection between research and practical concepts as superintendents takes both experience and experimentation, but can ultimately produce the most effective results. Hopefully the thoughts provided in this chapter will accelerate your wisdom and enhance your practice in the superintendency.

Chapter 3

Hiring, Supervising, and Mentoring Employees

A BRIEF STORY...

During Rhonda's many years in the superintendency, which included leading three different school districts, she had always sought to hire individuals with the best technical skill and experience. Hiring individuals with the greatest degree of technical competence made sense, and frankly this was the way Rhonda had always seen the hiring process work.

One day Rhonda read a business article that challenged the notion of focusing on hiring individuals with the best technical skill and experience for new positions. Instead, it urged leaders to set a threshold for acceptable skill and experience during the screening process and then shift the hiring focus to emotional intelligence and character, in other words assessing *organizational fit*.

In hiring for the next principal position in Rhonda's school district she tried this concept and found it yielded an individual who had the technical skill and background to be successful, but more importantly was a perceived to be a great fit for the organization. As Rhonda reflected back on previous hires she realized that when focusing primarily on skill and background she had often hired individuals who were ultimately difficult to work with or did not stay with the organization for an extended period.

The wisdom of making a shift in the hiring focus enabled Rhonda's district to develop a cohesive team that accomplished its goals on a regular basis, while at the same time reducing employee conflict and turnover.

INTRODUCTION

As superintendents we understand that it is the quality and effectiveness of our employees that provides the foundation for academic and operational success. Embracing this fact we must make hiring, supervising, and mentoring employees a top priority.

In this section an eclectic set of concepts are outlined that superintendents might not often consider, but can play an important role in the employee hiring and development processes. If we can hire well, effectively grow employees, and provide appropriate accountability, our districts will perform better both academically and operationally.

CONCEPT 16—TECHNICAL COMPETENCE VERSUS EMOTIONAL INTELLIGENCE AND CHARACTER

Most superintendents are inspired to establish a high-performing, student-focused culture within their organizations, and it is not easy. In most situations superintendents inherit a culture that, as we know, either assimilates all who enter or attacks them like a virus if they seek to promote change or create disequilibrium.

One of the best ways to impact the culture of an organization, although it will take time unless there is a high degree of turnover, is through thoughtfully designing the hiring process (much like Rhonda did in her district). Assuming adequate quality within the potential hiring pool, superintendents can have a great impact on the organization with a few key personnel changes.

As this is the case, it is very important to understand the technical competence versus emotional intelligence and character concept when selecting new employees, especially when those employees are administrators. Friend and business consultant Art Pulis talks about this point, and it makes good sense. Unfortunately, many of our organizations focus primarily on the candidate's skill set and background (technical competence), without adequately considering the components that impact the individual's long-term fit.

If superintendents are to impact the culture and character within their organizations, they must hire individuals who are aligned with not only the vision and mission, but also the culture and character superintendents hope to establish. To do so superintendents should absolutely screen for technical competence, but *hire* for emotional intelligence and character.

In other words, as long as individuals in the hiring pool exhibit a certain level of technical competence (skill and background), the superintendent (or hiring team) can then shift focus to the candidates' emotional intelligence and character *fit*. Technical competence can always be enhanced, but rarely can a new hire's emotional intelligence or character be changed.

Superintendents who screen for technical competence but hire for emotional intelligence and character will find that they can have a much greater impact on the organization. This concept seems intuitive, but often (for a variety of reasons) it does not occur.

Often the negative issues that superintendents deal with on a daily basis are a function of organizational culture. As leaders we must have a vision for the type of culture we hope to establish and diligently work toward achieving this vision with each and every hire we make.

Of course, this takes time, but with focused effort we can change our schools and districts for the better. Obviously, it is much easier when a new school is being established and the culture can be created from scratch, or when a district is fast growing and there are many opportunities to bring in new staff, but needed changes can come in established settings too.

Patience is the key, but with ongoing effort cultural transformation is possible and when it occurs, the positive organizational impact can be felt for decades. Superintendents who realize that this transformation is in large part a function of the individuals they hire and focus their selection processes on personality and character create an environment for excellence.

CONCEPT 17—MINORING IN THE MAJORS

Dale Knott, a friend, former boss, and mentor who served in the superintendency for close to two decades, would often say: "If you are minoring in the majors, you are majoring in the minors." He was indicating that if individuals spend their time focused on dealing with the little things, the minutiae, they will never address the big things. How very true.

In leading others this is a message we need to convey to bring clarity to their work. We oftentimes must help our administrators (and ourselves!) remember to keep the broader goals of the organization in focus. It is very easy for us as leaders to get diverted by the concerns of those who do not see the entire context in which decisions must be made, and we can easily end up off track.

One might think of administrative decisions from the paradigm of an individual simultaneously looking through all of the sections in multi-paned window at the landscape outside. In doing so the individual is able to see the *big picture* (Eller and Carlson, 2009) as they contemplate the decision that must be made.

Effective decisions require a *big-picture* approach where all perspectives and angles are considered. In most cases, others will not have this foresight because they only see through one pane in the window.

If leaders can imagine the limited view that comes from looking through only one pane in a multi-paned window, they will easily begin to understand how people arrive at their perspectives. To the extent administrators can assist constituents in broadening their view during difficult situations it can help others to understand the basis for why certain decisions are being made.

So, if administrators are to prevent *majoring in the minors*, it is of vital importance that they gain and maintain full view of that which sits outside the window as they operate on a daily basis and make *big-picture* decisions for the organization.

CONCEPT 18—CIRCUIT TRAINING (ADMINISTRATOR INDUCTION)

An effective local induction program is very important to the success of new central office administrators and principals alike. Well-designed induction programs, which are followed with fidelity, shorten the period the period in which individuals come up to speed within the organization or a new position.

Effective and well designed is the key, because many of us don't take the time to properly onboard new central office administrators and principals. Often we give them limited training, provide the keys to their office or school, and check in as we can throughout the year.

Our intentions are good, but the program falls by the wayside as the tyranny of the urgent consumes all involved. The problem is that without a well-defined local induction system (followed with fidelity), training becomes haphazard and disjointed, oftentimes being commandeered by those with an agenda or the time to promote their area of focus.

One method that can be effective in designing thoughtful, well-planned induction programs for new central office administrators and principals follows the concept of a *circuit training* system.

You likely understand the concept of circuit training from weight lifting and exercise. The individual goes from station to station as they complete various exercises and weight lifting routines.

Circuit training as a metaphor for the induction of central office administrators and principals is very similar. In essence, new administrators are scheduled to meet with their supervisor and separately with various departments (e.g., HR, curriculum and instruction, maintenance and operations) to gain information regarding how that part of the organization operates and how it interacts with their new role.

The supervisor and each department leader meet with new administrators, individually, and focus on key information in a tailored manner so that personalized learning occurs. In other words, the new administrators follow a *circuit* as they are inducted into the organization.

Although this may seem time-consuming, it is actually more efficient in the end. By taking a thoughtful, personalized approach, the induction process shifts from a passive method of providing one-way information to a process in which ownership occurs and individual context and background are considered.

Exhibit 18.1 illustrates an outline of the principal induction *circuit training* process. Each superintendent must consider the unique context of his or her district in designing this process, but a well-defined system can enhance the induction experience and reduce the incident of error, concern, or challenge as the first year progresses for the new administrator.

It must also be stated that there are many effective state and national programs for administrator training through organizations such as The School Superintendents Association (AASA), the National Association of Secondary School Principals (NASSP), and the National Institute for Student Leadership (NISL).

The focus in this section was on the circuit training system for *local* administrator induction, but again there are many wonderful programs and options that superintendents might consider for training their central office administrators and principals.

Exhibit 18.1 Circuit Training (Principal Induction Process)

The principal induction process is a year-long activity, which is aimed at ensuring that you become familiar and conversant with the district's vision, operations, and culture.

An initial meeting with the superintendent and various other district-level departments should take place during the summer. Frequent meetings with the superintendent or your supervisor should take place during the school year to discuss your transition.

Superintendent	Human Resources (HR)
• Vision, mission, focus statement	• HR handbook
• Superintendent philosophy	• Key personnel policies
◦ Principal philosophy	• HR processes and procedures
• Organizational efficiency checklist	Technology
• Three things teachers expect from you	• Technology policies
• Personal organizational techniques	• Troubleshooting and problem resolution
◦ Notebook, Evernote, etc.	

(Continued)

Exhibit 18.1 (Continued)

- Communication protocol
- District quick facts
- Strategic portfolio
- School improvement process
- Key sections of the policy manual
- Crisis management plan
- Superintendent expectations for principals
- Beginning of the year and ongoing expectations for staff
- Seat count procedures
- Principal entry plan
- The change process
- Leading teams
- Building leadership capacity within your school

Volunteer/Grants Specialist
- Volunteers
- Grant writing process
- Communications
- Website

Transportation
- Bus routes
- Student discipline procedures
- Field trip/activity/athletic trip procedures
- Trip requests
- Vehicle requests

Business Services
- Budget 101
- Procurement processes
- Finance system
- Fixed assets requirements
- Staff/student travel
- Cash/money handling
- Food service processes

Curriculum/Federal Projects
- Curriculum management system
- Data Dig info
- Federal programs
- Professional development
- Conducting walkthroughs
- PLC 101
- Horizontal and vertical teams

Maintenance and Operations
- School dude/maintenance requests
- Monthly meetings
- Division of duties between maintenance and operations at school custodial staff
- Review of custodial staff duties

CONCEPT 19—ESTABLISHING NEW OR REDEFINED EXPECTATIONS

Superintendents supervise a number of administrators and staff members, and on occasion, based upon an identified need, are required to set new expectations or to revise existing practices for their performance. Changes may range from modifications regarding how a particular task is handled by the organization to revising an individual's job description due to reorganization. The question is, how will the employee react and how might superintendents ease the transition to the new level of expectation?

First, it is important to understand that employees will react to a new expectation in one of three primary ways (see exhibit 19.1). Employees may choose to *accept* the new expectation and begin operating in a new way. Alternatively, employees may choose to *comply* with the new expectation, meaning that they will *do what they are told*, but not necessarily embrace the change. Or, finally, employees may choose *non-compliance* regarding the new expectation ultimately deciding that either they can politically block the new expectation, leave the organization, or are willing to be terminated rather than comply.

Clearly our goal is for employees to always accept new expectations, but that cannot happen without due diligence on our part. To achieve greater levels of acceptance among employees when setting new expectations, we need to follow a well-defined process.

The following is an outline of how this might be accomplished.

- *Reflecting on "The Why"*
  - If we are considering imposing a new expectation we must reflect on *the why*, making sure we are on solid ground, and then being prepared to explain our rationale. The days of "because I told you so" are long gone; the phrase may gain the superintendent compliance, but will never gain employee acceptance. Start by determining what is driving the new expectation. Is it borne out of providing better service to students or because someone is pushing for a change to make his or her job or situation easier? Is the change better aligning the position with the vision and mission of the district? Obviously this takes some analysis because it is not always readily apparent, but superintendents must understand *the why* prior to determining whether the new or redefined expectation should be pursued.

- *What's the Impact?*
  - Once superintendents determine that the why behind the new expectation is reasonable, it is important to shift to considering its impact. Leaders must think through how this new expectation will affect not only the individual employee, but also the broader organization in its operational function and politics. Is this the right expectation to set? Is this the right time to set the expectation? How will this new expectation impact the organizational culture? Did the superintendent seek feedback from others regarding the impact?

- *Establishing Rationale*
  - Based upon the superintendent's analysis of the why and the impact of this new or redefined expectation, one is ready to finalize one's decision

and establish a rationale for the shift. To assist in this process it is informative to consider the levers of change described in Concept 13. Employees will move along the continuum toward acceptance if they understand the reasons behind the new expectation and can resonate with the rationale regarding its pursuit.

- *Implementation*
  - Although superintendents have spent time reflecting on the process of implementing the new or redefined expectation, a lot is learned once it goes live. Be open to making adjustments rather than feeling that it will be deemed a failure to adjust various aspects of the expectation. Regardless of how much preplanning occurs there is likely always something that can be tweaked to make the expectation more effective for all involved. In other words be prepared to monitor and adjust.

- *Evaluation*
  - Remember to evaluate, as time progresses, how the new or redefined expectation is working. Often we shift an expectation to solve a perceived problem just to find out that another issue occurs. Remember: Organizations are a *system*, and therefore modifications to one aspect of the operation will impact another and so on. Employees will appreciate the fact that their leader reevaluates how the expectations are working and also that their superintendent is interested in receiving feedback. Ask them how it is going. Often employees can identify key issues, obstacles, or areas of progress.

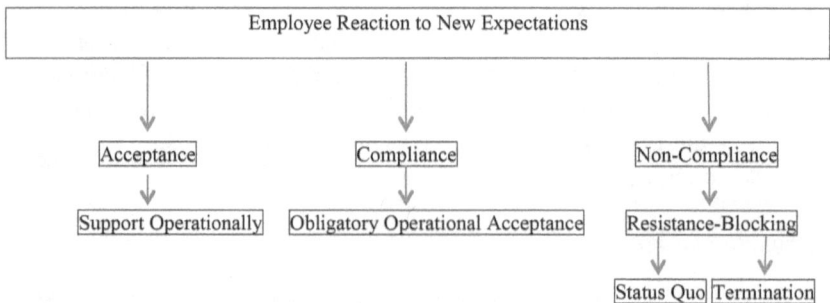

Exhibit 19.1 Employee Reaction to New Expectations

CONCEPT 20—EXPECTATION CLARITY AND COMMUNICATION FOR ADMINISTRATORS

We are often told that if we don't establish and maintain clear expectations for our employees, then they are left adrift like a rudderless boat. As this is the case we must create guidelines so the organization can run a charted course delivering the boat safely into the harbor.

Over the course of years, through trial and error, superintendents often labor to refine and make evermore concise the expectations that are imparted to their administrative teams. In this section the efforts of such refinements are distilled down to two primary documents, one outlining administrator expectations and one describing an administrative communication protocol.

The administrator expectations document that is provided has undergone years of refinement and is meant to outline basic guidelines upon which the administrative team should operate. Every superintendent will likely develop a variation of these expectations, which fit their leadership style and the school district context, but it is important to put some form of guideline in place.

These expectations should be developed in conjunction with the superintendent's cabinet and then refined as time progresses, but the design process is up to the district leader and must fit both their style and the context in which one works. Ultimately what is most important is that the superintendent and their team establish and operate under a clear set of expectations.

If the expectations are known and embraced, they place everyone on the same page, which preempts operational dysfunction, mismatched actions, and potential conflict among administrators and others. Exhibit 20.1 is an example set of these administrator expectations.

The second document discussed in this section is the development and use of a communication protocol. We all know that effective, timely communication is vital for administrators; in many cases it makes them or breaks them in their positions.

Again, like the administrator expectations document, a communication protocol ensures everyone operates following a common standard. The communication protocol superintendents develop should also be designed in conjunction with their team, once again ensuring ownership of the standards.

It should be understood that the document won't be redesigned annually, but it should remain in a state of adjustment as needs change, team members transform, or problematic issues are addressed. Exhibit 20.2 offers a sample communication protocol that can serve as a launching point for the development of a similar document in one's school district.

It does not take much to put a rudder on the boat and chart a course, but doing so will pay large dividends in terms of the consistency that is achieved among the administrative team. In school district contexts we often get picked apart when one administrator gets back to constituents within twenty-four hours and another does not do so for a week. Establishing clarity around these important issues for all involved enables the organization to run more efficiently and to minimize constituent complaint and concern.

Exhibit 20.1 Achievement Mountain Public School District Administrator Expectations

- Administrators will provide ongoing, close communications with their supervisor regarding projects, tasks, and duties.
- Administrators will answer e-mail and voice mail messages as quickly as possible, but no later than twenty-four hours.
- Administrators will seek guidance and advice from their supervisor on issues of importance and/or of political sensitivity.
- Administrators will be prepared to make recommendations on issues, but understand that he or she is expected to support the final decision made by his or her supervisor.
- Administrators will keep the superintendent apprised of communication with and/or from the school board.
- Individual administrators will always support administrative team decisions. . . . If an individual cannot do so publicly with his or her staff and others he or she should speak to his or her supervisor or the superintendent privately prior to taking further action.
- Administrators will follow policy and procedure without fail.

Exhibit 20.2 Achievement Mountain Public School District Administrator Communication Protocol

The following list outlines items to consider when communicating with others as an administrator in the Achievement Mountain Public School District. The list has been generated from information found in state statute, board policy and regulation, and cabinet-level administrative input. Although this is not an exhaustive list, it should serve as a guide to effective communication as an administrator.

- Seek to over communicate with your supervisor—When in doubt regarding whether to communicate regarding an issue choose to do so.
- Answer e-mail and phone communications within twenty-four hours, or the next business day, if over a weekend. Even if your message is short, it conveys that you received the message that was delivered to you.

- If considering a major change, decision, or action, communicate your thoughts with your supervisor. Bouncing ideas off your supervisor will lead to better communication and ultimately more effective decision making for the organization.
- If you have concerns, follow the chain of command in communicating your thoughts. As an example if an HR issue exists, start by communicating with the HR director. If the HR director gives you an answer that does not adequately address your concern, your thoughts should be communicated back to the HR director in an effort to seek resolution. If after taking this step resolution can't be achieved, let the HR director know you are going to take your concern to the next level in the organization. Once at the new level, follow the same procedure. If ultimately, resolution has not been achieved, follow board policy in moving your complaint to the school board level.
- When communicating concerns, be sure to use the *need-to-know* concept, which is borne out of the Family Education Rights and Privacy Act (FERPA). In essence, don't share issues with individuals who do not have a *need to know*. The reason for this approach is that it protects you as an administrator from confidential information being shared with third parties to the issue/concern.
- Review board policies regarding communication confidentiality. In addition, understand the components of the Public Records Act in relation to privacy and confidentiality of information.
- Remember that communication is a key component in the effective operation of an administrative team. The greater the level of appropriate communication between team members, the better off the team operates.

CONCEPT 21—SUPERINTENDENT/ADMINISTRATIVE ASSISTANT TEAM

Active superintendents understand how vital the superintendent-administrative assistant team is to the fulfillment of their position. An effective administrative assistant (i.e., secretary) takes on more routine aspects of work that frees up the superintendent's time to focus on more pressing and appropriate tasks. This can be a lifesaver.

An effective administrative assistant embodies four primary characteristics:

1) *The individual is trustworthy*. The superintendent can speak freely with and around the individual regarding confidential issues and know that the conversations will not leave the room.

2) *The individual exhibits high capacity.* In other words, if the superintendent is working on a presentation he or she can give raw information to his or her administrative assistant and the individual can pull something together for the superintendent in draft form, which one can then refine. Or if the superintendent needs a written report, his or her administrative assistant has the ability to start pulling material together and outlining the response, saving the superintendent time to reflect on the key points that must be discussed.
3) *The individual is an effective time manager.* Specifically, the superintendent's time is what is being discussed in this section. The best administrative assistants know when and how to place appointments on the superintendent's calendar, understanding the leader's work patterns, workload, and personal preferences.

Years ago there was a television series titled *MASH* about a mobile hospital unit that operated during the Korean War. The assistant to the colonel was affectionately called *Radar* because he knew what the colonel was thinking and was prepared with the necessary material before the colonel would verbalize his request.

It was funny to watch, but it exemplifies what is described here. If the superintendent's administrative assistant can accurately anticipate his or her boss's needs, it makes the district leader's job infinitely easier. Of course, to an extent this requires conversation and training regarding the superintendent's priorities, but in the end it is a skill that superintendents must look for when hiring an administrative assistant.

4) *The individual is an effective access manager.* The superintendent's time is so very valuable because once the district leader is in the office people, requests, phone calls, questions, e-mails, texts, and so forth come at him or her from every direction. If superintendents are required to handle every request for their time throughout the day they will end up *majoring in the minors* (see Concept 17), which means that the mission and vision (big picture) of the district will be left behind.

Savvy administrative assistants know how to handle the phone calls, requests to *pop in to see you*, meeting requests, sales calls, and so forth, but this does not happen without some training on the superintendent's part. District leaders must work with their administrative assistants to establish certain parameters.

As an example, if a parent calls to complain about a bus incident a treasured administrative assistant will determine whether the individual spoke to the transportation director or the principal first. The parent may not like the fact that he must follow the chain of command, but setting this standard encourages resolution of issues at the appropriate level and saves the superintendent time to deal with the concerns that should be addressed by the district leader.

Another example would be sales calls. The proficient administrative assistant will always take a message if a sales person desires to speak to the superintendent so that the superintendent can assess whether he or she is the correct person to speak to the sales representative and/or whether the district requires the type of service being offered at that point in time.

So, the goals as superintendent in this area are twofold:

1) During the interview process the superintendent must focus on analyzing and assessing how to establish a match between potential administrative assistant hires and the four characteristics listed earlier.
2) If the superintendent is coming into a new position that already has an administrative assistant in place, then the existing employee must be trained and mentored in the four characteristics. Of course, the first characteristic, trust, can't be trained, but it can be stated and expected.

Experienced superintendents will tell you that a highly effective administrative assistant is one of the primary keys to their success. Choose wisely and train diligently, because the board hired the superintendent to focus on moving the district to the next level and without an effective partner in that effort (the administrative assistant) it will be a very difficult task to complete.

CONCEPT 22—SUPERVISORY CONTINUUM

As evaluators of district staff (and likely principals too), we need to remember the importance of differentiation in the supervision process. It is likely that we are supervising a continuum of individuals from those new to their positions to seasoned administrators.

Regardless of the individual's background and experience (or time in the position) we must assess their ability to effectively fill their role in a manner consistent with the job description and our priorities. Remember: Beyond the job description, as superintendent, you may establish certain priorities that you deem necessary for success on your team. An example of this might be how administrators communicate with you or others within the organization.

So, we must place those we supervise on a continuum measured not only by their ability to do the job but also regarding their alignment to the priorities we wish to establish. To do this effectively, many superintendents have found Glickman's Supervisory Continuum to be useful (Glickman, Gordon, & Ross-Gordon, 2018) (exhibit 22.1). You will notice in the exhibit that the employee is placed on a continuum that impacts how the superintendent provides supervision and promotes professional growth.

The chart starts on the left side, describing a non-directive approach, and progresses on the right to a directive level of interaction and supervisory involvement. Thus, regardless of the individual's experience, if he is not currently successful with components of the job description or is not aligned to the priorities the superintendent is establishing, then he would start on the right side of the continuum. Employees placed at this point on the continuum are guided and mentored extensively so that growth and effectiveness can occur.

Alternatively, if superintendents supervise an individual who is both effective in fulfilling the components of her job description and shows alignment with the superintendent's priorities then she would be placed on the left side of the chart. As a supervisor superintendents would use the tight-loose leadership approach with her that is described in Concept 29. In other words, the superintendent would establish with her the goals to be accomplished, but give her freedom to complete the process as she deems appropriate.

In the middle of the supervisory continuum is the point at which superintendents would take a more collaborative supervisory approach. In this scenario, superintendents would work together with the employee to establish a process of identifying and achieving stated goals. The superintendent would encourage the employee and help him to reflect on the process that is developed, and assist him as he completes the work.

The supervisory continuum is an important tool to remember and to reflect upon as a superintendent. In many cases we use a singular approach in working with those we supervise, rather than providing the differentiation that is vital to their success.

Applying the supervisory continuum is intuitive, but like many of the concepts in this book, we must reflect upon how to be purposeful in its implementation and use. Doing so not only promotes growth in those who we supervise, but also encourages the priorities that we have established as superintendents.

1	2	3	4	5	6	7	8	9	10
Listening	Clarifying	Encouraging	Presenting	Problem-Solving	Negotiating	Demonstrating	Directing		

Non-Directive ——————— Collaborative ——————————— Directive

Veteran ——————————— Developing Professional ——————— Rookie

Aligned Organizationally ————— Transitional ——————— Individually Focused

Exhibit 22.1   Glickman, Gordon, and Ross-Gordon's Supervisory Continuum. *Source:* Adapted from Glickman, C., Gordon, S., & Ross-Gordon, J. (2018). *SuperVision and instructional leadership: A developmental approach.* New York, NY: Pearson.

CONCEPT 23—INTERVIEW QUESTIONS THAT REVEAL CORE BELIEFS

The hiring process is always a challenge in that school districts are attempting, especially when hiring key positions, to determine how the interviewee aligns with the organization and its beliefs. An extensive process is normally established to reveal as much about how the candidate thinks and operates as is possible.

One way to attempt to reveal a candidate's core beliefs and potential for strong organizational alignment is through the design of targeted, effective interview questions. In his book *Hiring for Attitude: A Revolutionary Approach to Recruiting and Selecting People with Both Tremendous Skills and Superb Attitude* author Mark Murphy (2016) outlines a system for designing questions that can provide important information about interviewees.

Murphy's system starts with determining a certain trait that is desired by the organization. As an example the district may desire an individual who will deliver high-quality customer service. Next, an open-ended question is developed that targets this trait, for instance: *Describe how a teacher repair work order would be handled from beginning to end.*

Once the question is established the *best answer* is developed, although Art Pulis, the business consultant mentioned earlier, extends Murphy's process by also determining what the *worst answer* might be in this situation. In other words, a continuum is developed with the best answer at one end and the worst response at the other. A rubric can easily be developed to make this process more clear for the interviewer with a five- or ten-point scale used depending on one's preference.

If quality customer service is a key trait for the organization, then a series of questions can be asked regarding this topic. Asking the question in various ways helps to confirm the conclusions that can be drawn from the interview process.

Thoughtful analysis regarding the traits required in key positions and the development of interview questions that reveal a candidate's core beliefs in these areas are important in establishing organizational alignment. Superintendents can never guarantee that those they interview and hire will *fit* the organization, but using Murphy's interview question technique they can reduce some of the risk faced.

CONNECTING THE DOTS IN CHAPTER 3

Hiring, supervising, and mentoring employees as stated at the beginning of this chapter is likely one of the most important things that we do as superintendents. School district budgets are typically 85 percent or greater employee salaries and benefits; therefore it is the quality of our personnel that drives our success.

As this is the case we must not only think through the types of individuals we should hire (technical skills versus emotional intelligence and character or superintendent-administrative assistant team), but also how we can guide them to be most effective (minoring in the majors, expectation clarity and communication for administrators, supervisory continuum or circuit training).

In addition, school districts are often faced with financial challenges, shifts in focus driven by state government requirements, or implementation of local initiatives. To effectively plan for and react to these changes superintendents must often reorganize or restructure the school district's staffing (new or redefined expectations) to keep the organization operating successfully.

Clearly there are many different facets involved in leading, organizing, and overseeing the school district's human capital. Hopefully the varied and unique concepts outlined earlier will drive your thinking deeper in terms of not only who to hire but also how to make employees more effective through training, supervision, and accountability.

Chapter 4

Leadership and Decision Making

A BRIEF STORY...

John was frustrated. Serving as superintendent of a mid-sized suburban school district, he found himself often pulled off course by employee issues, parent complaints, and events that were beyond his control. It felt to John as if he would start the week with focused intention, just to see his plans unravel by Tuesday morning.

One day, while meeting with a fellow superintendent over lunch, John described his issue in an attempt to commiserate and get the challenge off his shoulders. John expected to hear a *me-too* response from his friend, but to his surprise he was offered some wisdom on the subject.

John's fellow superintendent had served in some tough positions over the years and therefore experienced this phenomenon on numerous occasions. The wisdom he imparted changed the way John dealt with this challenge from that point forward in the superintendency.

First, John's friend described this issue as the *tyranny of the urgent*. John had heard this term before and understood that it meant leaders often get pulled off course by issues that are determined to be *urgent*, often by others, at the expense of priorities that the leader has set for themselves or the organization.

Next, John's fellow superintendent indicated that John should find a *visual reminder* to refocus his priorities on a regular basis. A visual reminder that had meaning and impacted John at a personal level would stand as a symbol of what John was hoping to accomplish.

John reflected on this concept and remembered a photograph he had of a former student in her cap and gown who graduated despite great adversity in her life. John posted the photograph by his office door so that he would see it every time he left his office. The photo stood as a reminder that John believed all students could succeed, and this core belief was the driving force behind the work he attempted to accomplish each and every day.

INTRODUCTION

The process of leading an organization and making wise decisions is not easy. We all receive training in these areas but quickly realize that the challenge is in how to apply what we have learned to a particular context. Decision making is oftentimes situational, and rarely do we operate in a context where black-or-white options are apparent.

Of course, there is information and wisdom we gain through experience, but anything we can do to shorten the path to greater understanding will be coveted. The hope in this chapter is to provide some of those shortcuts. Clearly this is not a tome on leadership and decision making, but rather a few concepts that upon reading and reflection might make your job easier.

CONCEPT 24—DECISIONS: I MAKE, I CONFER, I DELEGATE

Superintendents make hundreds of decisions each day, so it is important to reflect on how those decisions are approached and also who, if anyone, should be involved in the process. One framework to consider is stated in the title of this section: Decisions: I Make, I Confer, I Delegate.

The hope is that superintendents will see this framework on a continuum. In other words, there will be *Decisions I Make*, which require little to no input. Alternatively, *Decisions I Confer* are always informed by others. Finally, *Decisions I Delegate* will be for all practical purposes decisions that are passed on to others with minimal levels of monitoring and oversight. It is important to point out these nuances because as with most arenas in leadership, decision making is *gray*, as alluded to in Concept 25.

It is also clear that decision making and any framework to which superintendents adhere is very personal and will be a function of the individual's personality and leadership style. So, let's unpack these three areas a bit more and as superintendents reflect upon how we can tweak, modify, or change what has been outlined to create a personal fit.

Decisions I Make

The *Decisions I Make* typically fall into one of two categories:

1) The decision is routine or binary. In other words a routine decision would be one that is repetitive and normally made in the same manner. An example would be determining annually which communication methods will be used if a school closure is required. A decision on this item is typically consistent year after year.

A binary decision is going to require that a choice is made between two fairly clear alternatives. For instance, if the school district experienced a snow storm overnight, the superintendent must decide to either run school the next morning or cancel. The decision is black or white, either/or, and again, must go one way or another.

2) Alternatively, the *Decisions I Make* may relate to something the superintendent feels specifically responsible for and will own 100 percent. It is not to say that the superintendent won't seek guidance in making the decision, but he or she will make it clear that he or she feels the decision is his or hers to own; good or bad.

An example of a decision that a superintendent may make would be whether to conduct one administrative retreat or two. Superintendents may feel that they must own the decision based upon time available, content to cover, and so forth.

In some cases the superintendent's final decision will be in line with the general consensus of individuals involved throughout the organization, but sometimes it might be different. Superintendents know they have full view of the organization and must make decisions that take this unique perspective into account.

Superintendents also realize that it is important to communicate, up front, when an issue falls into this realm. If others in the organization understand that this will be a *Decision I Make*, it helps them because the superintendent is providing clarity from the outset. Superintendents often experience challenges when the types of decisions they are making are not stated, or are not clear to their constituents.

Decision I Confer

Superintendents strive to keep most of the decisions they make in this realm because it is typically best for the organization. It really comes down to the old adage that *two heads are better than one* when decision making is required.

Most superintendents put in place a cabinet made up of key administrators in the district for this very purpose. The cabinet serves three primary functions: (1) It provides thoughts, analysis, and feedback on issues so that the superintendent can make more informed decisions. (2) It is a group that often stands in alignment through making a shared or consensus-based decision on a particular issue. (3) It is an information dissemination group, which ensures that good communication is occurring between the district, its schools, departments, and other constituents.

The group is tasked with disseminating key messages and ensuring that *two-way* communication is occurring between the district and the various other parts of the organization and/or community.

Conferring on decisions can be done in a number of different ways organizationally. As stated earlier a cabinet group is a good vehicle for feedback, but town hall meetings, surveys, faculty meetings, and focus groups can also work well in certain situations.

The bottom line is that the more decisions upon which superintendents can confer the better off they will be as a leader, the more effectively the organization will operate. It is important that superintendents not get caught in the trap of believing that if they confer with others prior to making a decision they are weak or indecisive. In fact, constituents will see superintendents who confer as stronger decision makers. Superintendents are operating out of a data-driven decision-making paradigm as they collect both quantitative and qualitative information to inform their decisions.

In the end, when superintendents confer during the decision-making process, they are still making the final decision. Although these decisions will be more consensuses based, it will be the superintendent, as the organization's leader, who has reflected upon all of the data, information, and opinions prior to moving forward.

Decisions I Delegate

The *Decisions I Delegate* are important but tend to be related to items upon which superintendents can accept multiple outcomes. Superintendents delegate these decisions because they want the employee or group to be fully empowered in the decision-making process.

Superintendents may establish decision-making parameters and assist the group in assessing possible options, but ultimately they leave it up to the individual or group to decide. The key in this arena is that as superintendent one must accept any number of outcomes related to the decision at hand.

Decisions in this realm can run on a continuum from how the district's professional development room is designed and laid out to how the district will select next year's school calendar. Again, the decision is important, but it is not necessary that the superintendent, as the organization's leader, has the final say.

CONCEPT 25—LEADERSHIP IS GRAY

It is our natural inclination to see leadership and decision making as black and white, right or wrong, good or bad; but in reality leading others and making decisions is most often gray. Therefore, in most cases the direction we take on a daily basis as a leader or decision maker is not clear. It comes down to making a judgment call.

Superintendents can struggle with how to address an employee issue or whether to choose one alternative over another when all options seem to have equal value—and that's okay. Effective leaders realize that one's decisions, although typically anchored by deeply held principles, are always a function of the specific context and will be impacted by timing.

As an example, the decision to permanently close a school is never black or white, but rather a function of the unique set of circumstances and individuals involved in the process. It may seem logical to close the school for a variety of reasons, but the timing may not be right to gain sufficient support for the initiative. The question is, how do superintendents know whether the context and timing are favorable to make a certain decision?

Ultimately we can't, but we can use tools to assist us in making a more clear determination. Two tools proven helpful in this process, listed in Concept 14, are the Culture and Change Template (Exhibit 14.1) and the Windowpane Model for Analyzing Constituent Perspectives (Exhibit 14.2).

Although many decisions we face are not clear, we can attempt to make them a bit less gray. If we can analyze the potential success of our initiatives, we enhance our ability to make sustainable decisions as opposed to creating opposition. As leaders this should be our goal, but without thoughtful reflection and analysis prior to taking action we are unlikely to succeed.

CONCEPT 26—TYRANNY OF THE URGENT

How often do superintendents start off a school year with focused intention just to find themselves lost in minutiae, fighting fires, or dealing with issues outside their control? Most superintendents will indicate that they are not the only ones who have fallen prey to this challenge during their career, but rather it is a fairly common occurrence among K–12 administrators. The question is, how can superintendents maintain focus or, at a minimum, anchor themselves in such a way that they are drawn back to that which they deem important?

Many superintendents find that visual reminders make a difference. A visual reminder must be highly personal, meaning that it has a strong impact upon the leader once noticed. It must be both located in a place that easily catches the superintendent's attention and unique enough to stand out from the environment.

An example of this idea is the use of student portraits to create an emotional impact. Hanging directly across from one superintendent's desk, on the opposite side of the room, are two self-portraits: one of Jesus and the other of Priscilla. Jesus and Priscilla (see Exhibit 26.1) were third grade art students in one of the superintendent's previous school districts who produced wonderful self-portraits of themselves.

The superintendent was so impressed by their work that he purchased the portraits from the students and has used them ever since as a way to remember, on a daily basis, why he serves in the position. In spite of budget issues, crises, or other daily concerns, upon looking up from his desk he is automatically drawn to Jesus and Priscilla. It is their portraits that focus his work and help him to remember that although the tyranny of the urgent may be upon him, there is a much larger goal he is attempting to pursue.

Exhibit 26.1   Jesus and Priscilla

CONCEPT 27—ORGANIZATIONAL VIRUS

Superintendents, especially if they are new to the district, will be bringing about change within the organization. Existing superintendents are often involved in change processes too, although the reasons for the change will be different. The concept to convey in this section is that regardless of whether the superintendent is new to the district, or existing in the position, the change they desire to bring about will be treated like a virus.

Clearly this is a unique analogy, but the organization will treat change similarly to how the body treats a virus. Once a virus is introduced to the body, white blood cells seek to attack it in an effort to neutralize its impact. We are fortunate that our bodies work in this manner, but we must understand that organizational systems react in the same way, which can be good or bad depending upon the individual perspective.

The culture of the organization, like the body, wants to maintain equilibrium. It does not want to change, and if leaders don't recognize this characteristic, then their initiatives are doomed to fail. We also must understand that it is not the size of the change that initiates this response, but rather the fact that disequilibrium is being created.

So, whether superintendents are implementing a new time clock system, closing a school, or modifying the length of the school day, each of these initiatives will be treated the same way by the culture of the organization.

A key question is, how should superintendents design a change process within their organization to produce successful results? Many superintendents find that the ideas mentioned in Concept 14, models such as Howard Gardner's levers of change, and the notion of tying an emotional component to change initiatives work well.

Although we will not always be successful in introducing organizational change, understanding how the culture might react and what can be done to mitigate the effects of this reaction is of vital importance for us.

CONCEPT 28—THE BLUNT REALITIES OF LEADERSHIP

Some who are reading this book will either be considering a move into the superintendency or possibly have recently been hired into the position. Others may be current superintendents but have been thinking about the realities of their position and how these challenges can be managed.

Regardless, one thing that is hard for individuals to understand (or impart to others) is what it means to be the lead district administrator: to be the boss. As the superintendent of a school district, the axiom *the buck stops with you* becomes apparent very quickly. We train for this leadership transition, we watch and learn from others, but it is very difficult to truly sit in the leader's chair.

In this section we review some of the realities of being the lead administrator. Although what is outlined may seem daunting, do remember that being the superintendent also comes with many benefits. Experienced superintendents will likely indicate that despite the challenges, they enjoy the position and the opportunities afforded them to impact students' lives. So don't forget this lens as the issues outlined next are read and reflected upon.

A recent social media post written from the perspective of a head baseball coach, Mike Deegan, described the realities of being the boss and how the lead position differs in significant ways from serving as an assistant or other subordinates within the organization. An adaptation of a few of those challenges is outlined here, along with how each might be managed or potentially mitigated for lead administrators.

Leadership Is Lonely

It is true. The lead administrator or CEO has no peer within the organization, and according to coach Deegan, "there will only be a very, very select few people who know what you are going through" (Deegan, 2017). Active superintendents will confirm that while you can talk to others about challenges, frustrations, and dilemmas, unless individuals have been the leader of an organization, they simply can't conceptualize the realities of your situation.

As this is the case, we must seek out individuals who can serve as a sounding board. In most situations superintendents seek out colleagues in their position or other government agency leaders (e.g., city managers). Business leaders can understand some of what education leaders face, but typically they don't experience the same level of constant scrutiny from the public in their positions.

Leaders Get Questioned

One reality of being the district leader is that superintendents make decisions, and decisions have consequences. In subordinate roles administrators make recommendations, and although the recommendations may be accepted the fact remains that one does not take the heat if they go wrong; the leader does. People will often second guess the superintendent's decisions, especially with the benefit of hindsight. Leaders must be prepared for this reality and know how to react once questions emerge.

To prepare oneself for the reality of others questioning decisions it is important to remember three key points: (1) Superintendents can't get emotional or let their reaction erode their credibility, (2) superintendents must endeavor to slow down and reflect prior to making decisions so that wisdom and experience can guide their thoughts, (3) if superintendents make a mistake or miscalculation, then they should admit it, fix it, and move forward. Individuals who cling to bad decisions because they fear being judged as indecisive end up with greater problems in the long run.

Leaders Will Be Unpopular (But Hopefully Respected)

To lead in a moral and ethical manner means that at some point, with some individual or group, the superintendent will not be popular. The bottom line is that superintendents can't please everyone and if they attempt to do so they will be constantly blown around by the prevailing winds, which leads to burnout.

Superintendents must also establish a certain level of emotional distance from their leadership team and employees so that objectivity is achieved. Occasionally, administrators become too close to subordinates and when tough decisions are required they are deemed biased by others, or their credibility is put into question.

It is a natural tendency to want to be liked. Superintendents must understand this tendency but reframe their focus around a desire for *respect* as an alternative. To be respected we must operate from a predetermined set of core principles, a philosophy if you will (see Exhibit 28.1), which anchors our thoughts and actions when the winds of challenge blow. Superintendents who do so, over a period of time in their positions, gain respect. This should be one of our primary goals as leaders.

Although there are many blunt realities in leadership (and specifically the superintendency), the three listed earlier impact all of us. Whether we are new to the position or have served for an extended period, these realities will be faced by all. It is important for each one of us to reflect upon these realities and to think through how we will face these challenges as lead administrators within our organizations.

Exhibit 28.1 Superintendent Philosophy

As superintendent, I will:

- Strive to be a student-centered leader
- Focus on "constancy of purpose"; that purpose being to move each student to the next academic level
- Support a well-rounded student experience that values co-curricular and extracurricular pursuits in connection with academic excellence

- Hire people, not skill sets
- Collaborate in planning and decision-making processes
- Focus on analysis and next steps, not excuses and expect the same from others
- Exhibit a positive, can-do attitude
- Exhibit a high degree of professionalism and trust and expect the same from others

CONCEPT 29—TIGHT-LOOSE LEADERSHIP

The concept of tight-loose leadership is likely familiar to most reading this book, but it is important to highlight the idea here because it is fundamental to a successful superintendency. In working with one's board most superintendents have established a strategic plan, or some set of goals and objectives, which provide a path for the school district's ongoing improvement.

Superintendents are tasked with leading the organization toward achievement of these goals but must effectively employ the efforts of their leadership team, principals, and staff to experience success. Logically this is where tight-loose leadership comes in and why it is so important as a management process.

Superintendents must be *tight* (establish a high level of accountability) related to what will be accomplished, but they must be *loose* (open to varying methods) regarding how the task is completed (Peters & Waterman, 2015). The alternatives to this method of accomplishing the district's goals, while not good, focus either on micromanagement of individual details (which leads to burnout) or on a laissez-faire approach where no one is accountable for goal accomplishment (leading to organizational chaos).

Clearly, different goals must be handled in accordance with the situation at hand and in consideration of the personnel available (see Concept 22). The tight-loose leadership model is an effective tool for holding the organization accountable while simultaneously empowering others. Any time a superintendent can both accomplish the goals of the district and effectively engage others in the process, it is a win-win situation for all.

CONCEPT 30—ROOT CAUSE ANALYSIS

One of the biggest issues we face as educators is that the problems we attempt to solve are complex, multifaceted, and oftentimes partially outside our control. Compounding these challenges is the fact that school districts are typically understaffed and everyone is extremely busy.

So, when it comes to solving perceived challenges we often neither properly identify the problem nor fully research the solutions. We see another school or district trying a new technique and quickly move to adopt it without understanding the unique nature of how it might work in our context. Or we see a new tool or educational solution at a conference and purchase it as a way to solve a perceived issue. Neither of these options will enable us to develop a well-designed, sustained solution, and thus it is important to step back and think a bit deeper.

As the leader of the school district this is where root cause analysis (RCA) comes in (Barsalou, 2015). If we can discipline ourselves and our employees to use RCA when we have a problem, rather than jumping to conclusions, we will achieve much greater success in actually reaching a solution.

How often have we seen schools look at low state test scores, and without deep analysis do we draw the conclusion that the teachers are new, or the kids have learning gaps, or (you fill in the blank)? By short circuiting a full analysis of the issue we fail to drill down to the true cause of the problem.

By not understanding the *root cause*, our solutions can miss the target and thus we will enter a loop of applying a series of ongoing perceived fixes. Although we think we are addressing the issue, in fact we are addressing symptoms rather than the root cause.

RCA can be implemented in many different ways, but this example is limited to the *5 whys* concept. Most find this concept easy to use and in exhibit 30.1, a working example is provided to enhance understanding. In simple terms, the *5 whys* is a group process that enables leaders to distill a problem down to its most fundamental component. See the illustration that follow related to analyzing why student absentee rates are too high.

The group may not need *5 whys* to get to the root of the problem, but alternatively more may be required. Using the *5 whys* method tends to provide enough analysis to appropriately unpack the problem, and this is the reason it is used on a regular basis (Exhibit 30.2).

Most superintendents will have seen quick, underdeveloped, or perception-based solutions used over and over again in their districts. This is often an outgrowth of work volume and the perceived need for a quick solution. Superintendents must discipline themselves and their organizations to make RCA their first step in the problem-solving process. Clearly the better we understand the issues we are addressing, the greater the success will be in crafting effective, sustainable solutions.

5 WHYs Example

Define the Problem: Student absentee rates are too high.

Why is that?

1. Students don't care about school and are unmotivated to learn.

Why is that?

2. Students don't see relevance in what we are teaching.

Why is that?

3. Students don't understand how what they are learning will impact their lives.

Why is that?

4. We have not been using real-world applications in our instruction.

Why is that?

5. Our teachers have not been trained to tie their instruction to real-world applications and the use of examples.

Exhibit 30.1   Root Cause Analysis Example. *Source:* Adapted from: http://centreurope.info/5-whys-template-free-download/5-whys-template-free-download-root-cause-analysis-template-15-free-word-excel-pdf-documents/

CONNECTING THE DOTS IN CHAPTER 4

Ranging from decisions superintendents make to daily distractions to analyzing the root cause of problems this chapter covered a diverse set of leadership and decision-making concepts.

Unfortunately, although superintendents often confer with others in advance of making decisions, those decisions are rarely clear and are heavily impacted by context and timing. We must understand these facts to accelerate our wisdom and be clear regarding the many forces that can take us off track. It is also important to know that wisdom in leadership and decision making

5 WHYs Worksheet

Define the Problem:

Why is that?

1.

Why is that?

2.

Why is that?

3.

Why is that?

4.

Why is that?

5.

Exhibit 30.2 Root Cause Analysis Worksheet. *Source:* Adapted from: http://centreurope.info/5-whys-template-free-download/5-whys-template-free-download-root-cause-analysis-template-15-free-word-excel-pdf-documents/

requires us to be strategic and have tools available to successfully address the challenges we will face.

Leadership and decision making are challenging not only because of the contextual dynamics we face, but also because we must have the wisdom to make situational adjustments as issues arise. The goal of this chapter was to outline some of the leadership and decision-making issues superintendents encounter, but also to provide thoughts on how to address these tasks in a nuanced way.

Chapter 5

Politics, Legislative Influence, and Local Campaigns

A BRIEF STORY...

Makayla was new to the superintendency and had never really dealt with, nor understood, the political process. She served a board that expected Makayla to be involved at the state capitol, so she knew she needed to learn quickly.

The leader of one of the regional superintendent associations that Makayla belonged to had a long history at the capitol. Makayla reached out to her and asked if she could help her come up to speed regarding how to become politically engaged as a superintendent.

To start, the association leader told Makayla she needed to meet and get to know the legislative leaders who served her district. It was suggested that Makayla develop a brief *district profile* that she could share with her legislators, and then she should set up a meeting to get to know each individual.

Makayla followed this advice and set up a series of meetings where she introduced herself and shared the district profile with each legislator. She knew that her legislators were very busy, thus the one-page profile would be something that could be referred to in the future.

As the new legislative session was about to begin, Makayla reached out again to let her legislators know she could be of assistance when needed. Makayla provided her cell phone number and indicated they could call, or text, any time an issue required discussion.

Ultimately, after a few years of interacting with her legislators Makayla became *a key legislative constituent*, meaning whenever an education issue was before the legislature she would receive a call to offer thoughts and advice. Makayla's board was very pleased with what she had accomplished in establishing legislative relationships. Makayla had put the school district on the map that promised to pay ongoing dividends in terms of legislative influence.

INTRODUCTION

Today's superintendent must be politically active if they are to protect their district and promote ideas that will make learning more effective for their students. The level of political activity superintendents pursue will likely be based upon their interest, but may be driven by a specific need in their district.

In this chapter the hope is to provide some basic ideas regarding how superintendents can get to know their legislators, introduce them to their district, and establish a relationship designed to encourage ongoing support and involvement. In addition, local campaigns (i.e., levies, bonds, and overrides) will be discussed, and some thoughts regarding how to achieve success in this realm will be provided.

CONCEPT 31—DEVELOP A DISTRICT PROFILE

Legislators are busy, so any time superintendents meet with them, or provide a written communication, it must be brief and to the point. One idea that introduces legislators to the superintendent's school district is the development of a district profile (see Exhibit 31.1).

The profile is a one-page document (one side, not two) that provides some basic information about the district, so legislators serving the area have a quick reference when bills are proposed or questions arise.

In addition, the profile should outline key issues that the superintendent hopes will be addressed by the legislature during the upcoming legislative session. The document is quick for legislators to read and easy for superintendents to update. It provides important information and is memorable for both legislators and their staff members.

Exhibit 31.1 District Profile: Achievement Mountain Public School District Profile

Achievement Mountain Public School District Overview:

- Serves 1,500 kids in four schools (one of each K–5, K–8, 6–8, and 9–12).
- Covers 916 square miles primarily in Pine County, but a small portion in Aspen County.

- Has 237 employees (100 certified, 137 classified).
- Fifty percent of high school population comes from surrounding K–8 school districts.

Achievement Mountain Public School District Successes:

- Spruce High School was named a "model school" by the National Commission on Education and the Economy (NCEE) for its conversion to a whole school competency-based learning approach.
- Vine Maple Elementary was highlighted in *Time Magazine* for its implementation of the Knewton adaptive math program.
- Spruce High School was named winner of the prestigious Golden Bell Award by the Sky Island School Board's Association for its implementation of the Move on When Ready Program and the Big Sky Diploma.
- Achievement Mountain School District was the first district in Pine County to adopt open educational resource digital textbooks called FlexBooks.
- Fern Digital Learning Program was named as one of four national models for blended learning.

AMSD Challenges:

- Attracting and retaining high-quality teachers because of rural location.
- AMSD's capital budget has been reduced by 91 percent since 2008.

In addition, the profile should be placed on district letterhead so that the superintendent's contact information is readily available to area legislators or their staff members. It is also important to provide a business card with the superintendent's cell phone number. Legislators will often call superintendents on their way to another meeting, or even from the legislative floor while a discussion is taking place on an educational issue.

During the legislative session superintendents will want to be available on a moment's notice for their legislators as it may be the only opportunity to influence the writing of a bill, or to impact a vote.

CONCEPT 32—GETTING TO KNOW YOUR LEGISLATORS

It is very important to get to know the school district's legislators, but this can take a lot of effort. Again, legislators are very busy so superintendents need to bend their schedule around that of their legislators and find ways to pique their interest.

The following list mentions some of the methods superintendents have found to be successful in engaging legislators serving their school districts.

- Call your legislator's office and ask for a quick ten-minute meeting to introduce yourself and to provide a bit of information about your district. Once there, provide your legislator with the one-page district profile and speak briefly about the district, its needs, and its constituents (remember these are the legislator's voters). Also, in advance of the meeting, research the legislator so you know his or her key positions and can reference them positively or avoid certain subjects that might generate problems.
- Invite legislators to a well-attended school event where they can be visible to many and play an important (yet non-controversial) role. As an example, you may have a local science fair or spelling bee. Invite your legislator to be the one to hand out the certificates to the winners.
- Set up a meeting between your legislator(s) and your board to have breakfast so that a simple dialogue can occur. Make it a low-key event to ensure everyone gets to know each other and also to discuss your priorities, which were identified in your district profile.
- Give your legislator an award for his or her efforts to support your school district. If your legislator has supported a key bill that impacted the district, or the education community in general, invite him or her to a board meeting and give him or her an award. Remember Concept 25, the blunt realities of leadership? Well these issues impact legislators too. If your legislators has stepped forth to provide support for your district or education in general, they deserve your recognition. We all know they will hear plenty of negative comments about the work that they do, so your efforts to provide support will be memorable and will help to establish an ongoing relationship with your legislator.

These are just a few ideas, and seasoned superintendents can dream up many more, but the key is to get to know area legislators and help them better understand the school district they serve. Once superintendents have established this initial relationship, they are ready to move on to the next step, which is becoming a key legislative constituent.

CONCEPT 33—BECOMING A KEY LEGISLATIVE CONSTITUENT

Once superintendents have established a solid relationship with their legislators, as outlined in Concept 32, they are now ready to pursue becoming a key legislative constituent, which is where one's influence begins to create an impact.

A key legislative constituent is an individual who legislators will discuss issues with on a semi-regular basis. If a bill is before their committee and it contains a component that will impact education, superintendents want to be in a position where their legislator is calling or texting them for advice, or to discuss the bill's impact.

Legislators tend to only maintain a few key legislative constituents in important areas (e.g., education), and superintendents want to be a go-to person in their area of expertise when questions arise. Once district leaders achieve this status, they will be able to impact legislation and even propose ideas that might be crafted into bills. Key legislative constituents may also be asked to testify when a bill is before a committee.

Testifying is an interesting experience and once again enables superintendents to potentially impact the outcome of legislation that is being considered. It may be a bill that was written to address an issue that directly impacts one's district or a more broad concern, but regardless a district leader's efforts as a key constituent can create positive results for his or her students.

Establishing and maintaining one's status as a key legislative constituent can be difficult and time-consuming, but ultimately it is very important in the role of school superintendent. Unfortunately, much of what dictates the direction we pursue in education relates to initiatives from the legislature.

Without the assistance of key legislative constituents, legislators often vote on issues deprived of correct information, or may even be misinformed by special interest groups. It is our role as superintendents to fill this gap and to make sure the legislators who represent our districts understand the issues and vote knowing how each initiative will impact our students.

CONCEPT 34—LOCAL POLITICS

Superintendents who accomplish broad goals for their school districts have almost always successfully navigated the community's local political environment. It may be that funds are needed for a technology initiative and local foundations must be approached, or new teachers require housing options, or possibly a bond must be passed to repair roofs. In each of these scenarios superintendents cannot be successful without understanding and engaging in local politics.

In this section, local politics takes on a broad definition. Clearly there are the locally elected officials and CEOs from varying organizations that superintendents must be able to engage, but there are also other leaders (formal and informal) in the community who shape public opinion. Superintendents must be able to enlist the continuum of key influencers in their community to support and help promote important school district initiatives.

Superintendents accomplish goals within the local political context by forming relationships. Although this is somewhat natural based upon the meetings and events superintendents will attend, or the clubs and organizations they will join, it still takes ongoing and intentional effort.

Relationships come through communication with key influencers, getting to know them, understanding their thoughts about the local schools, assessing their support for the public education in general, and so forth. Partnership is established through being open and attentive to opportunities for collaboration. An example might be a local business that desires to provide food boxes for needy children during the summer, or a hospital that wants to send volunteers into an elementary school once a week.

Strong relationships and partnerships within the community provide a solid foundation for the support of school initiatives. The question is, how do superintendents start to make these connections a reality?

The first step in the process is to determine who the key influencers in the community are, regardless of whether they are in the formal (e.g., elected official or organizational CEO) or informal (e.g., anyone who shapes local public opinion) leadership structure. Once the key influencers are identified, superintendents must make an effort to form a professional relationship with these individuals. In the absence of establishing rapport with these leaders it will be impossible to tackle topics of importance to the school community.

Once the key influencers are identified, a communication strategy should be developed by the superintendent to keep these individuals informed regarding important school district information and marketing messages. One approach is to develop a quarterly newsletter that is sent to the school district's key influencers. A catchy name should be used (e.g., Champions for Children), and the communique should be directed at providing information the superintendent desires to have disseminated throughout the community. Of course, many different communication methods can be adopted, but the fundamental component is for superintendents to keep their key influencers informed and engaged.

Partnerships with other organizations in the community are important too. If the school district is seen as a good partner, and one that is willing to engage with other organizations, a synergy can be developed around support of the community's children. If the children are the focus, then as initiatives come forward from the school district such as bonds, levies, or overrides, the chance for support from other organizations increases.

Finally, an important takeaway is that key influencer relationships and community partnerships require an intentional effort to both establish and maintain. Although superintendents are pulled in many different directions and it may seem like missing various community meetings or events will be okay, they need to always think twice and assess the impact of their absence. Local politics, which are impacted by relationships, must be consistently measured if superintendents desire to accomplish the diverse goals of their school district.

CONCEPT 35—POLICY VERSUS POLITICS

In talking to legislators, superintendents will find that elected officials face a real dilemma when attempting to navigate policy versus politics. One must understand this challenge and realize it has an impact on what lawmakers can do, and thus what superintendents and their legislator might hope to accomplish during a legislative session.

The concept is that someone can have a great policy idea that he or she desires to bring forth, but if it can't be sold politically it won't go anywhere. Either the timing isn't right, it can't be sold to a majority of legislators, or modification may be required to gain needed support.

In these cases, the bottom line result is that although it may be a good idea it did not initially generate the necessary support to be successful. Unfortunately, politics is not always about good ideas, but rather negotiation, power, and timing.

At times the good idea put forth may get sacrificed for some other initiative, which has lessor value in our minds, but our legislator may feel it was necessary to achieve a bigger win on a different topic. We must understand and be prepared for these realities as we operate in the political realm.

Here is the good news: the legislative process occurs annually. As this is the case, it may take two or three years to get a good idea into law, but with hard work and lots of parent action, community support, and often state association backing we can potentially achieve success.

The goal in outlining the concept of policy versus politics is simply to remind superintendents, especially those new to the legislative process, that it is not always about good or bad policy ideas, but rather timing, connections, and ongoing hard work. Superintendents must evaluate the issues and use political capital wisely. If an idea is not going anywhere, it is not prudent to use one's political capital promoting it.

We may not be successful on the first try, but if we build coalitions around our initiative and make modifications based upon feedback, remembering that persistence is vital, we will ultimately have a better chance at success.

CONCEPT 36—LEVIES, BONDS, AND OVERRIDES

Every superintendent deals with, depending on the state in which they live, levies, bonds or overrides: in essence, local initiatives to increase school district revenue for a specified purpose. Over the course of history, superintendents have seen these campaigns go from very simple efforts to highly sophisticated processes designed by campaign consultants.

Successful superintendents become students of these processes and work to understand issues such as demographics, high-efficacy voters, marketing, targeted communications, and research related to campaign committee composition.

A helpful book regarding this topic is *School Finance Elections: A Comprehensive Planning Model for Success*, written by Don Lifto and Brad Senden (2010). In their book, Lifto and Senden discuss many of the topics listed earlier and provide an in-depth analysis of each so that districts can implement a well-designed campaign process.

In this section the goal is to point out a few key components that superintendents must know and understand when their district runs an election campaign. Although elections are typically very complex, hopefully this brief overview will outline a few points of vital importance.

Election Campaign Leadership Team

Research outlined in the Lifto and Senden book indicates that the election committee chairperson and leadership team can have a dramatic impact on a campaign's success. In other words, the individuals on the committee and their collective clout within the community make a difference. In each community there are individuals who are thought of as leaders and often shape public opinion. The extent to which these leaders are involved in the district's election campaign in a very public manner produces a positive outcome.

Lifto and Senden describe a novel way to recruit community leaders for campaign committees through the use of triangulation. Similar to the process used to confirm a finding in qualitative research, in this case Lifto and Senden identify three key individuals in the recruitment process: the individual targeted for recruitment, the superintendent, and a third individual who knows the targeted person on a personal level.

Using triangulation, the superintendent and the individual who has a personal relationship with the targeted person invites the potential recruit to lunch, coffee, and so forth. Once together, the superintendent explains the goal of the election campaign committee to the potential recruit and the individual who knows the person well confirms the importance of the group and the task at hand.

The idea is that although it may be easy to say no to the superintendent for political or other reasons, it is harder to turn down the individual with whom the potential recruit is well acquainted. Of course, the assumption is that the person assisting the superintendent in the recruitment process also plans to be involved with the election campaign, which adds credibility to the process.

Assuming the triangulation process works initially, then another community leader is targeted and assistance is requested from a new individual who can help with recruitment. The process replicates itself from there and this is how key community leaders are recruited to assist the school district with the election campaign.

One other important question that superintendents may ask is, how does one get the first person involved so that triangulation can occur? Of course, many creative methods can be used, but one of the easiest options is to start with someone the superintendent knows well and can readily recruit.

It may be someone from the superintendent's Rotary Club, Lions Club, or a leader who serves on a board with the district leader. Once this initial person is recruited, the process takes off from there.

It is also important to mention that there are likely community leaders who served on previous district election campaigns who will retain an ongoing interest. Oftentimes these individuals will have friends who might have an interest as well. Together, drawing upon previously involved community leaders along with use of the triangulation process ensures the best possible election campaign committee is assembled.

Know the Numbers

In an era of big data it is becoming easier to know who the voters are in one's district and to break down these data into many different subgroups. In all states superintendents can obtain a voter file through their local, county, or state elections office. This allows those involved to see how many eligible voters reside in the school district, what party they have chosen (Republican, Democrat, etc.), which elections they voted in recently, their age, their address, and more.

Understanding these data at the granular level is important because it provides the opportunity to analyze the characteristics of the district's voters and then to plan targeted messaging and marketing efforts that most effectively address voter concerns and desires. The more one knows and understands about local voters, the more effective one can be during the election campaign. Regardless of whether information is being disseminated from the school district itself or the election campaign committee, developing a well-defined voter profile is an important first step.

So, it is important to obtain the voter file and to develop a profile of your school district for use during the election campaign. Logically, this profile should be locally developed, based upon the unique characteristics of your district.

As an example, does the district have retiree communities within its boundaries? Do developments that primarily serve families with school-aged children exist? Do local voters tend to lean more toward Democrat or Republican? Is the median voter age on the younger or more mature end of the spectrum?

It is questions like these that must be asked and then analyzed to develop a profile that will inform the district's targeted messaging and marketing efforts.

Targeted Messaging

Today it is not uncommon to be working with four different generations (Greatest Generation, baby boomers, Generation X, and millennials) during school election campaigns, and therefore districts must differentiate their message based upon each group's concerns and desires.

In addition, districts may be working with concentrations of similar voters in certain precincts, such as those who live in a retirement community. Individuals living in a retirement community will vote much differently from parents of school-aged children. All of these dynamics must be analyzed and understood prior to beginning a school election campaign.

We must also know that older generations consume information more completely and likely in written or hard copy form (newspapers, brochures, etc.), while the younger generations look to social media and video with much less time on their hands.

Later in the book the concept of equitable versus equal treatment of school board members is discussed and the same principle applies here. We need to be equitable in providing information to the various voter groups, but that does not mean the information will be delivered in the same (or equal) manner.

Once the various groups and voter characteristics are identified, targeted messages can be developed, to include their concerns and desires, which will more effectively inform individuals during the election campaign.

An example may be that you have a retirement community adjacent to a family development and school. The families are concerned about their children's education, and the messages they receive about the election campaign will likely relate to hiring quality teachers, maintaining a strong curriculum, and so forth.

Alternatively, the adjacent retirement community may not be as concerned about teachers and curriculum, but rather their home values and the fact that good schools will bring more families, which will generate interest from grocery store chains and other retail businesses.

In essence, we must understand the voter data and study our community's characteristics so that we can effectively target messages that are meaningful to them and also promote our thoughts, ideas, and positions.

Campaign Marketing

As mentioned earlier, we are likely dealing with multiple generations among our school district voters. Each generation consumes information a bit differently, and we must understand and profile these characteristics if we are going to be successful in getting our message out during election campaigns.

It is also important to assess the marketing methods used during previous campaigns. Often, campaign committee members will want to look to what has worked in the past as methods to reuse in new campaigns.

In the absence of reflection and deep thought related to the current voter context, this can be dangerous because as time progresses and generations evolve what worked in the past may no longer be effective. Two commonly used methods from the past can be offered as an example in making this point, phone banks and neighborhood coffee group meetings, neither of which may be successful today based upon the changing nature of the electorate.

One way to generate support in the past was to use a phone bank. The campaign committee would find volunteers to make individual phone calls to people in the community to promote the election. Although this worked well in the past, it is likely now an outdated approach in most school district contexts. At this stage many people don't maintain a landline (preferring to use a cell phone) and simply don't want to be bothered in the evening by a phone call.

Also, it used to be that a successful method was to gather your neighbors to come hear a brief message about the election campaign over coffee, dessert, and so forth. Today most families are so busy with activities that they simply don't have time to attend.

There are likely other examples that superintendents can generate from past election campaigns in their own school districts, but the point here is that we must more fully understand how the generations operate today when developing our marketing techniques, rather than relying on successful methods from the past.

CONNECTING THE DOTS IN CHAPTER 5

An increasingly important part of the superintendency is one's ability to wisely navigate politics, legislative influence, and local campaigns. Polarization at the legislative level forces us to be aware of what is being proposed and to know how to have a say in the process. Equally important is to understand the local school district voter profile and deftly communicate messages to each group based upon their desires and needs.

It is not uncommon today for legislative proposals, which will have a dramatic impact on our schools, to come out of the blue. If we are not tracking these proposals in some way, and don't have a relationship with our legislators, bills can pass before we ever have time to understand the implications and take action.

To assist busy superintendents in tracking this important information they must remember to use the legislative services of their professional associations. Doing so provides one way to stay on top of what is happening at the legislature and refining the plethora of information one needs to know.

Local election campaigns are also a reality for every superintendent, although the process and terminology differs by state and district context. In this chapter, a few thoughts and resources were provided to spur thought and reflection as superintendents think about how to run campaigns, as well as how those campaigns have likely changed over time.

We are definitely seeing a shift in how we approach local elections based upon new technological resources and changes in how generations consume information. The continuum of individuals and preferences we must consider has never been more diverse. Tried and true campaign methods of the past must be reflected upon, and often new thinking is required to be successful.

The fundamental message of this chapter is that superintendents must realize political awareness and engagement are no longer secondary considerations in the position, but rather essential to the operation of our school districts.

Equally important is to fully understand the continuum of the electorate in our school districts and to develop messages and actions that speak to each individually. The days of a one-size-fits-all approach has passed, and this is noteworthy as we consider how to communicate with our constituents and plan our election campaigns.

Chapter 6

Mastering School Board Relationships

A BRIEF STORY...

Hector had worked with a number of board members during his career and always struggled with what exactly to provide them as part of the orientation process. The state association covered some topics, but there was a need for more in-depth information.

One day Hector read an article regarding the development of a *Board Orientation Manual* for new and existing board members. The manual was more clearly organized than Hector had provided in the past and covered topics that all board members face on a regular basis, such as handling complaints from the staff and public.

He ran it past the current board members for review during the annual retreat and then began using it as new board members were elected. The clarity it provided on a number of different topics was greatly appreciated by the new and existing board members. It really became an operating manual that all board members could use and refer back to as questions arose regarding their board service.

At one point Hector shared the document with a new superintendent in a neighboring school district and the concept grew from there to many other districts in his region. Hector was pleased, as was his board, and the manual became a tool that kept the board-superintendent leadership team on track and moving in the same direction.

INTRODUCTION

In this chapter we will focus on a few practical suggestions that can assist one in mastering the superintendent-school board relationship. It is important to note that working with a school board is as much an art as it is a science. It takes a high degree of emotional intelligence and skill in balancing multiple interests and needs simultaneously.

To a large degree, working with school boards is a function of our personalities as superintendents, the makeup of individuals on our board, what we find works (or doesn't work) as we gain experience, and the individual context in which we are serving.

There are certain common tenets that have been found to be effective in working with most school boards, but we must always remember that in the end it is the art of the relationship, in a particular context, that will enables us to achieve success.

It is important to point out that although school boards make decisions corporately, superintendents must be attuned to how they can assist individual board members in making an appropriate impact.

Individuals run for open positions on the school board because they want to make a difference. In most cases this is a noble endeavor, and the individual truly wants to assist the district in achieving its goals, but at times we encounter the single issue or micromanaging board member.

So, the key is to figure out how to simultaneously engage individual board members in appropriate actions, while maintaining their legally required corporate decision-making structure.

The goal in this chapter is to discuss these concepts and to provide some thoughts that can further superintendents' thinking on this topic. In addition, some practical tools are provided that can assist superintendents as they interact with their board members and seek to establish a healthy working relationship for all involved.

CONCEPT 37—MEANINGFUL BOARD INTERACTION

As superintendents we strive to maintain effective relationships with the boards we serve. To do this we must not only consider the corporate actions that board members are required to take in leading the district, but also how we can help individual board members make a difference.

Boards are tasked with setting goals, policy, and approving relatively routine processes, such as adopting the school district budget. Most board members have run for the board hoping to be more involved than just approving mundane matters at regular board meetings and therefore did not completely understand the role before being elected.

Clearly, this can be a challenge. The board's primary role is to provide high-level oversight, but most individuals did not get on the board understanding this reality. Many board members desire more. It is a struggle for some to follow the board's own policies regarding how the organization is to be run, especially those that relate to day-to-day operations. Again, these individuals want to make an operational difference, so a natural tension is created as result of the way the system is designed.

Setting goals, policy, and approving the budget does not feel as engaging or fulfilling as helping to determine how often the custodians clean the bathroom, or where the new school marquee will be located. Thus a dilemma is created.

Two ways to assist board members in balancing this tension are to: (1) assist individual board members in finding appropriate actions and (2) to treat board members equitably, but not necessarily equally.

An expanded discussion of these ideas, which can enable superintendents to more effectively deal with the natural tensions experienced with board member service, comes next.

Appropriate Actions

The concept of engaging board members in appropriate actions was briefly summarized in the introduction of this chapter. We must remember that board members come from a diverse set of backgrounds, and superintendents need to use this information in assisting them to find ways to become appropriately involved.

Some board members may have been mid-level managers in organizations, while others may have been self-employed. A few board members may have been former educators, and others worked primarily at the clerical level; very few may have experience leading a multimillion dollar organization.

It is this diversity that is both a challenge and an opportunity for superintendents in working with their boards. It is also important to be aware that most school board members' model for serving in elected positions comes through watching city councils or state and federal representatives. Most of these individuals are expected to respond directly to constituent concerns rather than encouraging individuals to speak to someone within the organization.

School districts are different in this regard, and it can at times lead to micromanagement. In most cases micromanagement "comes in two flavors—individual board members trying to solve problems for constituents, and board members individually or collectively trying to influence major management decisions" (McAdams, n.d.).

To engage board members in appropriate actions we must first understand their passions and desires as they relate to school board service. One individual may have a keen interest in the district's athletic programs, another in reading achievement, and a third regarding career and technical education. It is important to note that these individuals would not be considered single-issue focused, but rather during conversation and discussion it becomes the clear source of their interests and passions.

Once we understand individual board member interests and passions, we can find ways to appropriately bring them into conversations and planning that relate to these particular areas. It may be that we encourage their service on a committee, or gain their knowledge related to converting the soccer field from grass to turf; the idea here is that we draw upon their area of interest or knowledge to appropriately engage them so they feel they are making a difference.

Although this is a simple concept, I believe it helps to ease the tension that board members often feel regarding their constraints within the system. If individual board members feel they are making a difference, then the superintendent-board member relationship will be more effective and superintendents can assist board members in focusing on the big picture. In addition this technique helps the board to operate at a more functional level corporately because they feel the self-actualization of serving their community in a meaningful way.

To make this approach successful, the superintendent must think through logical boundaries and make sure the boundaries are understood up front so that the board member's actions don't devolve into micromanagement.

As an example, mentioned earlier was the concept of a board member researching the difference between grass and turf for the soccer field, which may be an area of interest or expertise for the individual. The key in these situations is to frame the expectation up front.

As an example superintendents may say: "I know you have an interest in this topic, and if you are researching the difference between grass and turf please send me your findings and I will pass that information on to the athletic director so she can include what you found in her report." Using this process the superintendent provided an outlet for the board member to play a role but also limited that role in an appropriate manner.

Equitable versus Equal

In *So Now You're the Superintendent!* (Carlson, n.d.; Eller & Carlson, 2009), and in subsequent writings for The School Superintendents Association (AASA) *School Administrator* magazine, the topic of equitable versus equal treatment of board members has been described.

It is important to return to the topic here because of its significance to the superintendent-school board relationship. The concept of equitable treatment focuses on the complex nature of what initially sounds quite simple.

Of course, we want to treat all board members the same, but we must remember that equal is not always equitable. In other words, the board member who travels each week and is away from home regularly will desire a different level of communication frequency than the retired individual who focuses on their school board service as one of two major life activities.

As such, superintendents must go through a process with individual board members of analyzing their interests, communication preferences, and level of desired communication frequency.

It may be this information is gleaned through face-to-face meetings, completion of a board member survey, or during a group planning process. Regardless, equal is likely not equitable for your board members. Each board member has different needs and desires, and thus successful superintendent-school board communication must begin with this understanding concept.

CONCEPT 38—BOARD GUIDANCE ON HANDLING COMPLAINTS

The issue board members will likely face most frequently, yet are least prepared to handle, is the challenge of addressing complaints. Complaints can come by phone, e-mail, at the grocery store, ball game, or other locations (Kaufman & Royer, n.d.). How can superintendents best prepare board members for these encounters?

Guidance offered by Kaufman & Royer through the Associated School Boards of South Dakota describes the use of the acronym LAST to address complaints. Listen to individuals, Acknowledge their concern, Send them to the correct person (which should be the lowest level in the organization where the issue can be resolved [e.g., teacher]), and say *Thank You*.

Outlining this process for board members can assist them in being prepared for the inevitable complaints they will receive. Kaufman & Royer go on to describe other important components of this process. As an example, the board's role regarding complaints is to be final decision maker at a school board hearing. Thus, it is important for board members not to engage in the process of reacting to the complaint (e.g., "I will check into it."), but rather to send it to the correct person so they remain fair and impartial.

Therefore, although it might be a natural human tendency, board members must refrain from agreeing with the individual lodging the complaint and abstain from making any commitments regarding potential action. Board members will need to be careful not to act as a mediator, advocate, or investigator, all of which can jeopardize the perception of their fair and impartial position.

Receiving and reacting to complaints will be an ongoing issue that board members face. To the extent superintendents can assist their boards through outlining and discussing the LAST complaint process, it can ensure issues are addressed properly and without complication.

CONCEPT 39—THE BOARD OPERATING PROTOCOL

Establishment of a board operating protocol (see Exhibit 39.1) is important so that the board and superintendent can identify key operational tenets that all understand and the board commits to follow.

Some states include, as part of their board policy, a code of conduct or code of ethics, which are similar to what is described here but typically tend to be more generic. Regardless of what it might be called in your district, a vital factor is that the document includes issues of importance for one's particular school district context.

The state school board association generic document (if one exists) may be a fine starting point, but likely a local discussion and adaptation process should occur for the protocol to have true meaning. School boards and superintendents who grapple with the issues important to them while developing a protocol more closely follow its precepts.

Superintendents must also be diligent to keep the document fresh by placing it before the board on an annual basis. Each year at the board's organizational meeting (when officers are chosen) the group should reaffirm the board operating protocol and signify so by signing the document individually. If the group wishes to modify the document at that point in time, they can do so or select an alternative time to take on that task.

Superintendents must remember that adherence to the board operating protocol is often aspirational for board members. In other words, although the board commits to following the protocol, there is typically no legal or policy-related recourse if that does not occur.

If superintendents encounter a context where there is a contentious board, or members who have chosen rogue actions, it would be best to discuss with the group (either on your own or through a school board training consultant) what sanctions might be appropriate to impose if the protocol is violated.

Action regarding any sanctions will need to be governed by the board as a whole, but as a precursor to more serious steps the board president can intervene. Intervention strategies can run on a continuum from a private conversation with the challenging board member to discussions with the district's legal counsel.

Of course, unless there are serious issues, most boards will shy away from discussing how they might sanction their individual members. Although this may be the case, the fact that a board operating protocol is in place and the group revisits the document on an ongoing basis normally works well for most school districts.

Exhibit 39.1 Board Operating Protocol: Achievement Mountain Public School Board Operating Protocol

For the purpose of enhancing teamwork among members of the board and between the board and administration, we, the members of the Achievement Mountain Public School Board, do hereby publicly commit ourselves collectively and individually to the following operating protocol:

- Surprises to the board or the superintendent will be the exception, not the rule. There should be no surprises at a board meeting. We agree to ask the board president or the superintendent to place an item on the agenda instead of bringing it up unexpectedly at the meeting;
- Communications between staff and the board are encouraged. However, board requests that will likely require considerable time or have political implications are to be directed to the board president and/or superintendent. All personnel complaints and criticisms received by the board or its individual members will be directed to the superintendent;
- The last stop, not the first, will be the school board. We agree to follow the chain of command and insist that others do so. While the board is eager to listen to its constituents and staff, each inquiry is to be referred to the person who can properly and expeditiously address the issue;
- As a parent, a board member retains the right to express his or her own personal opinions in verbal and/or written form;
- A board member will not solicit an issue, become a ball carrier for others, or work around administrative employees and will encourage others to present their own issues, problems, or proposals in a constructive manner;
- The board will emphasize planning, policy-making, and public relations rather than becoming involved in the management of the schools;
- The board will address its behavior by yearly self-evaluation and by addressing itself to any individual problems, such as poor meeting attendance or leaks of confidential information;
- The board will set clear goals for themselves and the superintendent. The board and superintendent will set clear goals for the Achievement Mountain Public Schools;

- The superintendent is the chief executive officer and should recommend/propose/suggest on most matters before the board;
- Individual board members do not have authority. Only the board as a whole has authority. We agree that an individual board member will not take unilateral action. The board president will communicate the position(s) of the board on controversial issues;
- When board members serve on various school committees their role shall be defined by the board as silent observer or active participant;
- Conduct at a board meeting is very important. We agree to avoid words and actions that create a negative impression on an individual, the board, or the district. While we encourage debate and differing points of view, we will do it with care and respect to avoid an escalation of negative impressions or incidents. Individual members may disagree with a board action, but will support the decision of the board as a whole;
- To be efficient and effective, long board meetings must be avoided. Points are to be made in as few words as possible; speeches at board meetings will be minimal. If a board member believes he or she doesn't have enough information or has questions, either the superintendent or the board president is to be called before the meeting;
- Board meetings are for decision making, action, and votes, not endless discussion. We agree to move the question when discussion is repetitive;
- The board will not play to the audience. We agree to speak to the issues on the agenda and attend to our fellow board members. Facts and information needed from the administration will be referred to the superintendent;
- The board will represent the needs and interests of all the children in the Achievement Mountain Public Schools.

Board President   Board Member

Board Member   Board Member

Board Member

Date

Copyright © 2009 by Corwin Press. All rights reserved. Reprinted with permission from *So Now You're the Superintendent!* by John Eller and Howard C. Carlson. Thousand Oaks, CA: Corwin Press, www.corwinpress.com.

CONCEPT 40—RESPONDING TO BOARD MEMBER REQUESTS

It is normal for individual board members to ask questions of the superintendent, to clarify positions, to provide parent/community feedback, and so forth. It becomes a problem when either individual board members make requests that require excessive levels of staff time or their concerns become micromanaging in nature.

Superintendents need to be careful in this area because the desire to be responsive can lead down a path of unrealistic expectation by individual board members. We all want to be seen as responsive, but to prevent the issues described in this section it is important to consider standards that address these concerns in the board operating protocol.

One important standard to establish with board members is when superintendents receive an individual request or question, they will provide a response to the entire group. In other words, although the request or question comes from one board member, the superintendent's response will be sent to the entire board. Superintendents who follow this standard cut down dramatically on time-consuming requests and micromanaging because often the individual board member making the request does not want the entire board to know about his or her demands.

A second (but related) standard might be to establish guidelines regarding which individual board member requests or questions will be addressed without full board approval. The standard in the previous paragraph required that individual board member requests be communicated to the entire group, but this standard focuses on the point at which requests will require corporate board approval prior to being pursued.

Some requests may simply take too much time or not be of great importance to the board as a whole. To address this concern, it is necessary to have a guideline that establishes the difference between those requests that will be automatically answered by the superintendent (and reported to the entire board) and those requests that require full board approval prior to being researched.

The conversation surrounding this issue and the related outcomes are strongly linked to the particular board the superintendent serves and the local school district context. Although we might be guided in this area by work completed in other districts, ultimately these are very local decisions.

It is also important to point out that superintendents must use a certain level of common sense and discretion regarding the standards listed in this section. Often these standards will be developed and implemented only when dealing with a dysfunctional board.

Although we should report the findings of questions posed by individual board members to the entire group, we must not carry this to an absurd level. In other words, if a board member desires to know where to pick up a high school sports schedule, that may not be of interest to the entire board. Conversely, if a board member is interested in an update on a current student discipline investigation that would likely be of interest to all.

The second standard, related to when to fulfill a request or seek corporate board approval, is rarely needed and tends to be very situational. Although engaging the board in establishing a standard preemptively is a good idea, typically this is a concern only when you have an unreasonable board member who desires volumes of information or staff time to conduct his or her duties.

CONCEPT 41—THE FRIDAY UPDATE

The Friday Update is a commonly used board communication tool for superintendents, and although it will go by different names in different districts, the concept is ubiquitous (see Exhibit 41.1).

Superintendents use the update to provide their boards with highlights from the week, which might include narratives, pictures, or videos. Superintendents also use the Friday Update to communicate information related to issues of importance at the local, state, and national levels.

It could be that the city is changing building codes that would impact the district, or that the legislature has put out a report on education funding, or possibly that the U.S. Department of Education has communicated new rules that will impact the career and technical education program.

As a way to keep the board generally aware of the superintendent's schedule, a bullet point list of the meetings attended is often provided. Finally, superintendents will regularly attach an article that will appear the following week in a local newspaper related to school district news, or provide some other form of media involvement or update (radio, TV, etc.).

While the Friday Update can be used as a mechanism to communicate with the board on a number of different issues, superintendents must always remember that this is a public document and thus is not a privileged communication to the board. If an individual completes a public records request asking for the Friday Update communication, that information must be provided.

Most already know about the concept of a Friday Update board communication, but what many may not have thought through is how to effectively manage its production. Superintendents often spend years scrambling on Friday afternoons, pulling together the information required for the update after attending to the details of their day.

As such, completion of the update becomes a harried process that is not only stressful but also leads to errors or a failure to include all that was intended. To be seen in a positive light by the board and to convey a sense of professionalism, other methods must be considered.

Wise superintendents realize that if they start the Friday Update on Monday and add to it throughout the week as events arise, it not only is more complete, but will for all intents and purposes already be finalized by the time they hit Friday afternoon.

Experienced superintendents also realize that rather than authoring all aspects of the Friday Update themselves, they can ask their administrators to provide a paragraph or written document related to an important issue. Although the superintendent may need to tweak the paragraph or document a bit to better meet the board's need for information, the time savings can be very beneficial.

Finally, some superintendents have delegated production of the Friday Update to their communication specialist (if they have one), which is a real time savings. The challenge with this option is that superintendents then abdicate what will be communicated to the board on a weekly basis. Not everyone will deem the same issues of equal value, and the tact with which they communicate the information will not be the same.

In addition, superintendents may want to communicate information that would not be shared with other members of their staff. Of course, it must be realized that the Friday Update is a public document, but that does not mean its contents are shared broadly on a weekly basis.

As this is the case, superintendents tend to personally prefer to produce the Friday Update themselves with information gleaned from others, or control its production in a tight manner. Clearly this is a personal decision for each superintendent and in part is a function of their individual context, schedule, and so forth.

The main point here is that it is important to have a weekly board communication, and secondarily that it can be produced in a variety of ways depending upon the superintendent's preferences and the school district context in which they work.

Exhibit 41.1 Friday Update: Achievement Mountain Public School District Friday Governing Board Update

Pearville

I met with the superintendent from Pearville today and he indicated that they plan to begin keeping all of their students in district beginning the 2019–2020 school year. At this point I believe we serve around 240 students from Pearville and their absence will have a dramatic impact on our school district programming. We likely will need to reduce many of the "additional" programs that we now offer. One comfort is that Pearville indicated they will "phase out" their students, which means the decrease would come over a four-year period.

Time will tell if this comes to pass, but it will require a well thought out plan to determine how to proceed.

Newspaper Editorial

I spoke with the publisher of the newspaper today and indicated that I would write an editorial regarding the state of school funding in our state. There is considerable discussion taking place across the state regarding the impact the current fiscal crisis is having on public education.

District Duties

At this past board meeting Jane Doe brought up the level of work being done in the district. There is a lot going on with all of the initiatives we have in place, but these efforts must be sustained if we are going to move student learning to the next level.

Although we don't have the financial resources to add additional staff at this point in time, I have begun to delegate some duties and am working on a reorganization plan. On Wednesday I met with John Buck, Ed Deer, and Red Doe regarding our efforts as a district office "team." As a result of this meeting, a few changes are being implemented that I have outlined below.

- John Buck
  - Volunteer program coordination
  - Financial management
- Ed Deer
  - K–5 curriculum coordination and professional development
  - Textbook purchase coordination
  - Benchmark assessment coordination
- Jane Doe
  - Prop 196 regarding teacher salaries
  - 6–12 curriculum coordination and professional development
  - Educational technology oversight

Again, this is a start to some of the changes I will be making, but I will present a full plan to the board sometime this summer. John, Ed, and Jane have been great in supporting the district's efforts so please give them a "thank you" next time you see them.

HR Process Revamp

We have been working on a number of revisions to our hiring processes and forms, which are borne out of the recent hiring issue. We are revamping all of our applications and adding a new one (coaching—paid and volunteer), developing both a candidate and HR application checklist, designing a volunteer handbook, aligning HR processes with current policy, adding policy exhibits where they are absent, and so forth. Much work is going into this project by district staff, and once complete I will share it with the board in its entirety.

Week's Highlights:

- Met with John and Ed regarding the CAILL Framework
- Conducted an administrative meeting on Tuesday
- Met with Ms. Blue regarding Friends of Music
- Met with Bjorn Jones and Jane regarding our new educational technology efforts
- Met with Rand McNally regarding Rand's expedited resignation
- Attended the Chamber After Hours Mixer at Clancy's Cycle
- Met to revise our HR processes
- Met with the superintendent from Pearville
- Met with the Exeter science teachers regarding the textbook adoption
- Met with Ron regarding moving Lisa out of the music room and transferring choir and band into that room off of the gym
- Attended the drama program's dinner theater at EHS
- Template Source: Wickenburg Unified School District, Wickenburg, AZ

CONCEPT 42—NEW BOARD MEMBER ORIENTATION

Superintendents should develop a procedure and specific documents to guide the new board member orientation process. A board orientation manual can be easy to put together and provide information necessary to quickly bring new board members up to speed within your school district. The state school boards' association will also provide orientation trainings, but typically these events address the broader concepts and legal requirements of serving on a board.

One does not need to start from scratch in developing a board orientation manual because there are typically examples available in neighboring school districts. If a sample cannot be found, send an e-mail to hcarlsonthesupt@gmail.com, and a sample template will be provided to you.

The orientation process can operate in group form, if there are a number of new board members, or individually if that is the superintendent's preference. Many superintendents, regardless of how many new board members may be coming on at a particular point in time, prefer individual orientation meetings. The advantage of the individual meeting is that it provides superintendents the ability to get to know the new board member a bit more readily and opens the opportunity for one-on-one dialogue. Clearly, the group meeting is more efficient, but this hinders the ability to establish strong individual relationships.

The following is a list of noteworthy items that should be included in a board orientation manual. The list is not meant to be all inclusive, and it is important to remember that documents such as this manual should be context specific.

Sample Board Orientation Manual Table of Contents:

- Vision, mission, and core beliefs
- Strategic plan and goals
- Current state of school district (academic, operational, current issues)
- District organizational chart
- Board operating protocol and policy related to board member ethics, conflicts of interest, and so forth
- Roles: Board members and superintendent
- Board meetings
  - Sample agenda
  - Roberts Rules of Order
  - Regular board meetings, special meetings, emergency meetings, study sessions, and executive sessions
- Board evaluation
- Superintendent evaluation
- Board member interaction with the public
- District spokesperson
- Confidentiality
- Handling complaints/concerns from staff and the public
- Requests for information
- Visiting schools
- Communication with school district staff

- Policy adoption and revision
  - Accessing policy online
- Annual organizational meeting
- Education acronyms
- Meeting with education services department and business office
  - Review standards, curriculum, and instruction
  - Review budget and finance procedures

Superintendents who spend time up front getting to know new board members and provide them with a well-designed orientation manual decrease the potential for issues and challenges as the transition process occurs. We must remember that most new board members have never served on an elected board and often do not have prior board experience at any level. As such, developing and implementing an effective orientation process can be helpful for all involved and provide a guideline upon which to operate.

CONCEPT 43—BOARD RETREATS

School boards tend to participate in one to two retreats per year. Planning of the retreat typically falls to the superintendent and board president, although all board members should have an opportunity to provide thoughts and feedback regarding the items to be discussed.

Board retreats are necessary events from the perspective that an extended time period is provided (typically one full day) for discussion and a more conversational approach is embraced. Some superintendents prefer to have board retreats facilitated by an outside source, especially when a contentious atmosphere exists at the board level, although the more common scenario is that the superintendent, often with other senior-level administrators, facilitates the process.

The question for many superintendents is how to structure the retreat so that key information is communicated, but there is plenty of opportunity for board member interaction and discussion. One approach is to break the retreat into segments. It is important for the board to discuss key topics and to consider goals for the coming year, but an opportunity to reflect upon the previous year, the district's current state, and its ongoing challenges are important too.

One approach is to start the retreat by discussing the past year's successes and to ask the board to add to the list. By framing the initial conversation in the retreat around the previous year's successes it creates a more optimistic environment for the day's activities.

Next, it can be helpful to focus on where are we now. Prior to setting goals or identifying areas for improvement a baseline needs to be established. The board's improvement efforts should be borne out of this baseline, rather than anecdotal thoughts or ideas.

To the extent the board can discuss the following types of topics during the where are we now portion of the retreat, it can provide focus for all involved:

- How are we doing in relation to the goals set in the strategic plan?
- How are we performing academically?
- What is our financial and enrollment forecast?
- What feedback are we receiving from teacher, parent, and student surveys?

At this stage a discussion related to the strategic challenges that the district might face over the next year should occur. Each year these challenges will shift a bit and should be reviewed so that board goals and planning not only consider the district's current state, but also where the district is likely headed.

The final stage of the retreat then focuses on the development of goals for the coming year, or adjustments required to the strategic plan. As a result of the discussions that occurred earlier in the day, the board should have a solid foundation for discussing where it wants to go in the coming year.

So, to review, by breaking the board retreat into segments superintendents can provide a foundation for the discussion of goals that are then borne out of data and strategic thought as opposed to subjective concepts, thoughts, and ideas. The key, regardless of retreat design, is to ensure that district goals are a function of thought and reflection prior to development and implementation.

CONNECTING THE DOTS IN CHAPTER 6

Mastering school board relationships is what separates tenured superintendents from those who are short-lived in the position. As stated in the chapter the superintendent-school board relationship is an art. Some individuals have the emotional intelligence and wisdom to survive and others do not, but all can succeed with training and experience. The concepts outlined in the chapter are but a glimpse into some of the methods that can be used to establish and maintain a healthy relationship with one's school board.

As with many aspects of the superintendency, the superintendent-school board relationship is highly contextual. Seasoned superintendents have often worked with multiple boards and can confirm that each is different and operated with a unique culture.

Learning and being attentive to the context, establishing jointly developed protocols, enhancing communication, and meeting the individual needs of each board member help superintendents effectively master the relationship that can make or break their career.

Chapter 7

Living the Superintendency

A BRIEF STORY...

Transitioning from the superintendency in one urban school district to another, Maria quickly assessed that she needed to begin by focusing on her life balance and health. In her previous position she allowed herself to become overwhelmed with the 24/7 aspect of her job and therefore she was not eating right nor sleeping well, and her family relationships were suffering as a result.

Maria happened to come across a post on LinkedIn that spoke to the issues of life balance and health for leaders, and it provided some helpful insights. As a result of reading the post she set up routines for her sleep; started eating in a healthier manner; and began her morning with a time of reflection, journaling, and study.

The results paid huge dividends in Maria's life. She found herself happier, more productive at work, and in greater alignment with her family. At points in time when it was appropriate, Maria would share the wisdom of these life changes with those she mentored in leadership and the superintendency.

Maria had become an advocate for establishing a strong life balance and health program in the lives of those in stressful positions, and she was often called upon by the state superintendents' association to speak on these issues. Maria's message was clear, if you want to help your organization move to the next level, you must first care for yourself. The message Maria conveyed resonated with many she came in contact with, and thus it became clear to her that to live the superintendency meant one must find life balance and health.

INTRODUCTION

The superintendency is highly complex, and the dynamics of the job should be thoroughly understood and reflected upon by those in the position. As we enter the superintendency, or change positions, we must not only understand our individual characteristics, but also what the school boards we will work for desire. Obviously this analysis is not easy on either end but must be thoughtfully considered if *fit* is to be achieved.

This chapter is an overview of some of the research-based challenges (potholes and pitfalls) faced by superintendents, and how each issue can be addressed through proper diligence. Also we review the different types of superintendent roles and how to assess each for personal alignment. Effective entry plans, life balance and health (an oft overlooked component of the superintendency), when to leave a position, and school district branding and social media are discussed, too.

Hopefully the concepts in this chapter will assist superintendents in better understanding this complex and multifaceted position and enable each individual to reflect both on themselves and what is required to achieve and sustain success in this unique role.

CONCEPT 44—FOUR SCENARIOS

A former superintendent colleague, Jim Rickabaugh, once explained that he believes there are basically four types of superintendent positions. If superintendents reflect upon this idea, they will likely determine he was very perceptive in his assessment.

Jim pointed out that when we enter superintendent positions, boards desire one of four scenarios: (1) The board wants someone who will bring a new direction to the district, (2) a superintendent is desired who will maintain the status quo, (3) an individual is being sought to implement the board's new direction, or (4) the board is searching for a superintendent to establish a broadly developed consensus-based direction for the district to pursue.

To be successful superintendents, we must work quickly to assess the school district context because when we enter a position, whether new to the superintendency or as a seasoned professional, we must determine which scenario the board is operating under. Oftentimes the board does not clearly state its operational preference and in fact may not have previously considered this question at all.

Typically boards spend their time, in conjunction with the search consultant, focusing on the traits preferred in the next superintendent or the issues they desire to address as part of the transition. The four scenarios are rarely considered and thus likely will not be communicated.

As a result, candidates, or newly hired superintendents, must then focus on the following questions to ascertain which of the four scenarios the board desires:

- Does the board want the new superintendent to come in with a plan?
- Does the board already have a strongly held position regarding next steps?
- Is it expected that a consensus-based process be pursued prior to moving forward?
- Although the board has listed various issues to address, are these considered tweaks, or wholesale changes?

Failure to clearly understand which scenario the board desires can lead to strife and place one's superintendency in jeopardy. So, to clarify which scenario is desired by the board the solution is quite simple. Ask!

Ideally, as the search progresses, attempt to determine the preferred scenario through conversations with the search consultant and the board. If not during the search, then clarify early in the transition stage with the board (more on this in Concept 45) as the entry plan is developed.

The reason for establishing clarity as early as possible relates to personal fit for the superintendent and board alike. Hopefully we know enough about ourselves to understand who we are and how we match the four scenarios. Although for inexperienced superintendents it may not be completely clear, for seasoned individuals it should be easily understood.

We need to know enough about ourselves to understand which scenario(s) we will thrive under and which do not fit our personality or leadership style. In other words, if one is a change agent and leading organizations through the change process is what energizes one then maintaining the status quo would not be a good fit. Filling a position where an individual does not fit can be harmful to the organization and to the individual's career.

It is important to begin by reflecting on our personal characteristics and preferences to more clearly understand which of the scenarios might be the best fit. Once this is accomplished we can then enter the job search focused on analyzing the type of situation we might be entering. Matching who we are to the job and the board we will be serving is of great importance and should be our number-one priority.

CONCEPT 45—ENTRY PLANS

Regardless of whether we are entering the superintendency for the first time, or switching positions, it is always wise to have a well-designed entry plan. The plan should include board input prior to implementation, and be designed to cover between a ninety-day and six-month time period. Effective entry plans are designed to provide the superintendent opportunities to listen, survey constituents, review important documents, and gather information regarding the culture. Ultimately, superintendents can triangulate these data to determine the current state of the district and assess constituents' aspirations for its future.

In Concept 44 we discussed the *four scenarios* and the fact that the situation superintendents are entering may not be completely clear to them. In most cases you will gain some level of understanding regarding which scenario you are entering through the search process, but this view may not be complete. During the entry plan phase you should be able to gain a comprehensive picture of the situation because you are studying the organization at a deep level. The direction you take based upon this information will be well informed and likely much more clearly aligned to the district's needs and desires (Exhibit 45.1).

Exhibit 45.1 Entry Plan Template: Achievement Mountain Public School District Superintendent Entry Plan

Outcomes:
- Gather information about the community and the organization in a systematic and thorough manner;
- Assess the system's strengths, challenges, and opportunities;
- Identify and prioritize critical issues;
- Create a network of contacts and resources

Board Activities:

Task	Constituency Group	Timeline
Review roles and responsibilities of the board and superintendent (review operating protocol)	Board and superintendent	July
Clarify the board president role as compared to the entire board	Board and superintendent	July
Establish an entry plan with input from the board and others	Superintendent, board, and others	July

District Office Activities:

Task	Constituency Group	Timeline
Clarify roles and relationships of district office employees	Superintendent and district office staff	May, June, July
Determine current organizational and operational norms	Superintendent and district office staff	May, June, July

Task	Constituency Group	Timeline
Meet with key district office personnel (CFO, HR, federal programs, special ed., technology, communications, etc.)	Superintendent and others	June and July
Meet with each operational department: food service, transportation, bldgs. and grounds	Superintendent and various department staff	July and August

Building Administrator Activities:

Task	Constituency Group	Timeline
Discuss school improvement plans for the upcoming year	Superintendent and school principal	June and July
Discuss last three years of assessment results and any other pertinent data	Superintendent and school principal	June and July
Discuss current status and focus of strategic plan	Superintendent and school principal	June and July
Gain understanding of each school's context: academic, cultural, and operational	Superintendent and school principal	July
Listen to key issues and concerns school faces in the coming year	Superintendent and school principal	June and July
Listen to how the work of principals can best be supported	Superintendent and school principal	June and July
Distribute entry plan survey to gather information on the operation of the district	Superintendent and school principal	July
Conduct administrative retreat to establish rapport, procedures, and expectations	Superintendent, principals, and other administrators	July

Student Activities:

Task	Constituency Group	Timeline
Establish Superintendent's Student Advisory Council	Superintendent and student leaders	August, September, October
Listen to issues that are important to students	Superintendent and school leaders	August, September, October

(Continued)

Exhibit 45.1 (Continued)

Teacher Activities:

Task	Constituency Group	Timeline
Understand structure, membership, and responsibilities of teacher groups (collaboration process, grade-level teams, department teams, committees, etc.)	Superintendent, teachers, and building administrators	September, October, November
Distribute entry plan survey to gather information on the operation of the District	Superintendent and teachers	August and September
Visit each classroom during the first two days of the school year	Superintendent and teachers	August

Parent Activities:

Task	Constituency Group	Timeline
Establish relationship with school-related organizations	Superintendent and parents	August, September, October, November
Engage parents at different school activities to elicit their hopes and dreams for the district	Superintendent and parents	August, September, October, November

Community Activities:

Task	Constituency Group	Timeline
Gather perceptions of the school district from within the community	Superintendent and community members	July, August, September, October, November
Establish opportunities to listen to various community groups	Superintendent and community members	July, August, September, October, November

Feeder School District Activities:

Task	Constituency Group	Timeline
Meet with feeder school district superintendents	Superintendent and feeder district superintendents	July, August, September, October, November
Determine how feeder districts are preparing students to enter high school	Superintendent and feeder district superintendents	July, August, September, October

Data Collection Methods:

- Identify and interview key community members and personnel (listed below)
- Review data related to student achievement and student activities
- Visit district schools
- Analyze written survey response data using Wordle
- Individual and group discussions

Interviews to Be Scheduled/Individuals to Meet:

- Board members
- Building administrators
- CFO
- Federal programs director
- Special education director
- Maintenance and operations director
- Communications director
- Curriculum director
- Technology director
- Athletic director
- Association presidents
- Community:
  - City officials
  - Police chief
  - State representatives
  - Service organizations
  - Clergy
  - Select community leaders (list developed in consultation with board)
    - Jeff Edwards—Town Manager
    - Jane Ress—Chamber Director
    - Roberta Strauss—Performing Arts Center Director
    - Ron Jones—Former Mayor and School Bd. Member
    - Jose Cantu— Mayor
    - Kristi Levin—Councilwoman
    - Elizabeth Redkin—Former Bd. Member and Levy Chairperson
    - Rick Johnson—Former Bd. Member
    - Kelvin Rosen—Editor, Local Newspaper
    - Debbie Elliot—Former Editor Local Newspaper and Levy Comm. Member
    - Ariel Ross—Former Superintendent
    - Bill Torgerson—Real Estate Broker and Developer
    - Barbara Wandling—Attorney, Former Council Member and Sch. Bd. Member
    - Helen Dierks—Former Councilwoman
    - Jerry Lowe—Businessman
    - Don and Maureen White—Parents of School-Aged Children
    - Lon Carlton—Businessman
    - Duane Lane—Clergyman
    - William Keller—Businessman
    - Tom Merino—Police Chief
    - Errol Lang—Elks Lodge
    - Cindy Ramsey—Rotary Club
    - Art Brown—Consultant
    - Ed Green—Former H.S. Principal
    - John Hedges—Former Bd. Member
    - Laura Cooligan—Former Bd. Member
    - Fred Langston—Private School Principal

(Continued)

Exhibit 45.1 (Continued)
Document Review:

- Strategic plan
- District budget
- District financial audit
- Salary schedules/placement guides
- Administrative procedures
- Board policies, regulations, and exhibits
- Administrator job descriptions
- Key personnel evaluations
- Content standards, curriculum maps, and pacing guides
- School improvement plans
- Student and faculty handbooks
- Federal grants and other funded grants
- Capital improvement plan
- Technology plan
- Crisis management plans

Emerging Issues:

- Levy election in November
- Organizational efficiency at high school level
  - Financial procedures
  - Student discipline
- Balancing the next fiscal year's budget
- Curriculum, assessment, instruction, and leadership next steps

Source: Adapted from Westbrook Public Schools, Westbrook, CT.

Exhibit 45.2 Entry Plan Survey Template: Achievement Mountain Public School District New Superintendent Entry Plan Survey

Hello! I am asking all staff members to complete this simple survey so I can gain a better understanding of the district; its positive aspects, opportunities, and challenges. My goal is to learn as much about the district as possible so I can develop a comprehensive entry plan. New superintendents often develop an entry plan to focus their transition efforts and help them come up to speed with what is happening in the district.

Please Check One Category:

Certificated Staff   Classified Staff   Administrative Staff

Questions:

1. Please describe the culture of your school and the district.

   School:
   District:

2. What are your hopes and dreams for your school and the district?

   School:
   District:

3. What is going well at your school and in the district?

   School:
   District:

4. What aspects of your school or the district might benefit from change?

   School:
   District:

5. What expectations do you have of me as your new superintendent?

   School:
   District:

6. General Comments:

   School:
   District:

CONCEPT 46—POTHOLES AND PITFALLS

In *So Now You're the Superintendent!* (Eller & Carlson, 2009), we described a research project conducted by twelve professors of educational administration called the *Beginning Superintendent Study*. The study was turned into a book by Carolyn Hughes Chapman titled *Becoming a Superintendent: Challenges of School District Leadership*, which outlines potential potholes and pitfalls in the superintendency (Chapman, 1997).

It is important for us to study the challenges that we as superintendents face as a way to prevent repeating the lessons that history can teach. It would be unfortunate for us to step in a pothole, but devastating to fall into a pit! The list that Chapman presents in her book (a partial adaptation is provided later in the section) is not just for new superintendents, but for all who serve in the position. In fact, the list can inform the practice of many of our central office and school administrators too.

Below each pothole or pitfall a reflection component that outlines thoughts related to the identified issue is provided. In addition, a few lines are offered for superintendents to write their own reflection, based upon their experience, background, and thoughts.

Superintendent Pitfalls

- Unshared Vision: Failure to recognize the *human side of the change process* and get stakeholders engaged in helping to determine the direction of the district.
  - Reflection: In part this issue is described in Concept 14, but the challenge is how to balance the need to develop a *shared vision* with the acceptance of research-based best practices that the organization may not want to consider, although will likely be vital to its success.
  - YourReflection: _____

  _____

  _____

- Too Much too Soon: Assessing problems too quickly and moving forward without broad understanding or support.
  - Reflection: Again, this item is discussed in Concept 14, but many superintendents find this issue a real challenge. As *early adopters* and *change agents* many superintendents can tend to move too quickly. To combat this concern superintendent's must work with their staff to develop a written proposal, allow all to vet that proposal, discuss the identified issues, and build a guiding coalition to sell the change. Following this process helps superintendents to slow down and ensure they have thought through most of the necessary challenges that might be faced.
  - YourReflection: _____

  _____

  _____

- Promises: Making hasty or baseless that work to compromise credibility.
  - Reflection: In Concepts 7, 8, and 13, this problem is discussed but the bottom line is to remember we must always seek to buy time when faced with proposals and questions. We must remember that what we say is often consumed as fact, regardless of whether we are talking conceptually on a topic.
  - YourReflection: _____

  _____

  _____

- Offending School Board Members: Not recognizing board members' need to feel important and failing to develop sound working relationships with them as individuals.
  - Reflection: In Concept 37, the practice of equitable versus equal treatment of board members is described. School board service is not always fulfilling because it is not an individual, but rather a group endeavor. If you can find areas of individual interest for your board members and help them to develop an appropriate avenue for that service, it can make a real difference for them as individuals.
  - Your Reflection: _____

  _____

  _____

- Not Doing Homework before Board Meetings: Failing to do the *behind-the-scenes* work needed to prepare between meetings.
  - Reflection: Superintendents are so very busy on a daily basis, and the board packet includes such extensive detail that a plan must be developed to ensure their homework is completed. Clearly you will need to go over the development of the board agenda with your administrative assistant and with the board president, but a review of the packet should be completed with each board member too. We can typically anticipate questions that might arise and thus it is important to spend extra time on those particular topics. Another technique that can be helpful is to review board presentations with the cabinet team to complete a *dry run* prior to the board meeting. Doing so provides the opportunity to hone the information and delivery, organizing what will be said rather than leaving the presentation to chance.
  - Your Reflection: _____

  _____

  _____

- Power Politics: Failing to take time to understand the various power groups and their agendas.
  - Reflection: Regardless of whether we are new to a position, or in an existing role, politics must always be understood related to how it impacts the actions we take. Power politics does not need to change the actions we

contemplate, but we do need to understand how it will impact the strategy, tactics, and timing we consider as part of the process.
- Your Reflection: _____

_____

_____

- Blunt Talk: Forgetting that diplomatic speech may be required when addressing organizational limitations or problems to avoid alienating people in the school district.
  - Reflection: Let's expand this reflection beyond just blunt talk to idealizing previous school districts or other contexts. Both issues can be a problem. Regarding blunt talk we need to remember that it is rarely what we say, but rather how it is said. Also, the idealization of previous school districts or other contexts can alienate people too. In both cases (blunt talk and idealization) we need to remember that although people may realize change is required, to undercut their competence, knowledge, background, or history works to alienate.
  - Your Reflection: _____

_____

_____

- Alone at the Top: Underestimating the complexity and loneliness of the position.
  - Reflection: In Concept 28, some of the blunt issues faced in leadership are pointed out that are not just faced by those in education, but business and other sectors, too. The fact that superintendents are the CEO of the organization and thus have no equal can feel isolating. Superintendents need to find time to interact with others in like roles, whether those individuals represent education or other employment sectors. The ability to share common issues, concerns, and effective solutions can be very helpful for all individuals who serve as the leader of an organization. Remember these are key roles professional associations provide; networking, job alike discussion, and interaction.
  - Your Reflection: _____

_____

_____

- The High Cost of Saving Money: Instituting measures to save money that end up not appropriately dealing with the situation at hand and create the need to revisit the problem within a short period of time leading to issues of animosity and lost credibility.
  - Reflection: School districts almost always lack adequate resources, regardless of the context in which they operate. Thus, saving money is a value that is broadly shared by the school board, community, parents, and staff. The problem is that superintendents can be enticed to *save money* through solutions that ultimately are not well thought out or researched and can lead to additional work or cost. Although it takes more time, successful superintendents develop processes by which a full analysis is conducted prior to making spending decisions. The concept of *quality* is frequently considered by effective superintendents, too. In other words a cheaper solution may exist, but the life cycle and thus the return on investment (ROI) is significantly less. Finally, financial decisions should be strategic in nature, which at times means they can look to be counterintuitive. As an example, the state cuts kindergarten funding to half day, but as superintendent you recommend maintenance of a full day kindergarten program. Financially this may seem counterintuitive, but strategically if you end up gaining more kindergarten students because neighboring districts cut their programs to half day the decision will be deemed both strategic and financially savvy.
  - Your Reflection: _____
  _____
  _____

CONCEPT 47—SUPERINTENDENT MENTORSHIP

Regardless of whether you are new to the superintendency and are looking for a mentor, or are a seasoned superintendent who desires to serve in a mentorship role, this section provides thoughts to consider. Being mentored, or serving as a mentor, requires much more wisdom than most individuals contemplate.

Mentorship requires alignment, fit, and dedication by both parties. We often hear of situations where a mentorship relationship did not go well. The reasons might be lack of care in pairing individuals, misalignment of contexts, or failure of one side to put in the effort necessary to ensure success. The goal of this section is to provide ideas to ensure mentorship programming stability and effectiveness.

The following is a list of items that should be considered by both mentors and mentees in advance of entering into a superintendent mentorship program.

Look for Someone You Can Trust

Above all, trust on both sides of the mentor/mentee relationship is vital. Superintendents must be able to place confidence in the ideas that are shared back and forth, and conversations should flow comfortably and suggestions should resonate. Agreement surrounding the concept of confidentially is also important. Both sides, the mentee and mentor, will likely share information that is highly personal, and any breakdown in confidence can be devastating.

So how do you assess for trust? Most superintendents have good intuition when it comes to other people, but when you interact with potential mentors/mentees look for openness, honest communication, and a spirit of support.

Also, do your homework. What do you or others know about the person's history? Do they exhibit moral and ethical character? What is their general reputation? Ultimately, trust your intuition and choose wisely.

Look for a Match in District Size, Complexity, and Needs

If the mentor/mentee relationship is to be enhanced, it is important to match the context in which the individuals work. This can best be achieved if the individuals face similar challenges in the superintendency. In other words, although a suburban superintendent working with a rural superintendent may work, it likely won't be as successful as the pairing of two suburban superintendents, or two rural superintendents.

Factors to consider include district size, student demographics, curricular alignment, board makeup, geographic location, and any other issues that may make the contexts unique. Aligning contexts can strengthen the relationship and provide a solid foundation for understanding between mentors and mentees.

Look for a Situational Match

Examine the major issues that the mentee will be facing, and assess whether these challenges have been addressed previously by the mentor. If the mentee's employee contracts have not yet been settled, a good mentor may be someone who has dealt with contentious employee negotiations. If the mentee's board needs support to become effective as a decision-making body, a good fit might be someone who has solid experience with board development.

Alternatively, a good match might be aspirational-based. As an example, possibly the mentee's district desires to implement a one-to-one laptop program. If the mentee can find a match with an experienced superintendent who has been through the process, a solid relationship can likely be established.

So, studying the mentee's situation and the mentor's experience is a good starting point for establishing a relationship.

The mentor/mentee relationship is must be reflected upon and entered into only after thoughtful consideration. Not everyone is meant to be a mentor, and not every pairing makes sense. It is only through open, honest conversation, reflection, and in-depth analysis that superintendents should ever enter into a mentee or mentorship role.

CONCEPT 48—LIFE BALANCE AND HEALTH

The longer superintendents serve the more they realize how important life balance and health are to success in the position. Some superintendents are very diligent to maintain a proper work balance and good health, but frankly they are in the minority—the extreme minority. Of course, we all make individual choices in this regard, but we must remember that as a superintendent we are always *on call*, and often the issues we face were not solvable by others.

The demands never end, and the complexity is at times unfathomable, although it is only a small number of individuals who understand this fact. Most superintendents never get a sick day; although they may truly be home sick, much of their time is spent addressing organizational issues and answering questions.

Vacations too, most superintendents can't recall a vacation with their family that was free of school district emergencies, issues, or challenges requiring their attention. In essence, unless one draws a line, they will work fifteen hours a day, six to seven days a week, which is neither healthy nor sustainable.

Oftentimes this is a choice. Yes, the job is very demanding, and if we want to be successful, we need to work hard and be prepared to face multiple issues and challenges on a daily basis. But, if we are going to sustain ourselves to meet the job's demands over the long term, we must achieve a level of life balance and health that will enable us to keep going, prevent burnout, and maintain our family relationships.

Although many superintendents are on a journey toward better life balance and health, which takes discipline, time, and reduced levels of stress, most are nowhere near where they might hope to ultimately be in their lives.

Regardless, it is possible to distill the basic issues that superintendents must master down to four areas of focus.

The four are not new, nor is this an expert analysis regarding how each should be addressed, but the point is to get started on the journey and to understand how superintendents might work toward a lifestyle that is sustainable and keeps them resilient.

Sleep

As superintendents most of us don't know much about this topic, but many have learned over the years that we must figure out how to get adequate levels of quality sleep to handle the demands of the job. This is something that each individual must figure out for themselves, but regardless it must become a priority.

If it is not a priority, we will note a difference in our performance and personal relationships. Although we may get away with a lack of sleep for a period of years, this does eventually take a toll on us and our families so establishing healthy habits early is of vital importance.

There is a lot of information out there regarding sleep hygiene, patterns, and so forth, but each of us must determine what it takes to find success in this area individually. Again, a lack of concern in this area can lead to deleterious effects in one's overall performance.

Eating

The problems many superintendents face related to eating are the irregular nature of their work schedule and the stress levels that are faced on a constant basis. It may be that they have a week where they are in lunch meetings every day and the next week they only have two lunches scheduled. Alternatively, a superintendent may be stuck in meetings all day long and does not have time to eat a particular lunch, or possibly they are going from a busy day of meetings to more school activities at night with no time to eat dinner until 9:00 p.m.

The schedule described here for superintendents is not unique but poses a real challenge for us in terms of eating healthy. Consistent with other items in this section it really comes down to discipline.

If superintendents force time into their schedule to eat and spend time preparing healthy food and portions, *and* don't reach for chocolate or sweets during stressful encounters, or during celebrations, they are headed in the right direction. No one is saying it is easy, and many personally find this to be the hardest problem to overcome, but we do know that it will pay dividends if we can make it work.

We are all creatures of habit, and if we can figure out a healthy diet that we can stick to on a regular basis, we will ultimately experience success. As stated earlier for many of us this is our toughest journey, but we also realize that we can positively impact our work performance and our lives if we can find the discipline to be diligent in this area.

Exercise

Most superintendents find that they must either set aside time in the morning to exercise or it does not occur. Our days are too unpredictable and if we think we can carve out time after work we are likely deluding ourselves. Most information we read about exercise indicates that if we set aside thirty minutes a day for physical activity at least five days a week, we become much healthier.

It is important to note that the superintendency, as a unique job, creates specific challenges that should impact our exercise choices. Superintendents sit a lot—truly a lot! We spend most of our days in meetings and the meetings require sitting. We sit in different types of chairs, in different positions, and in different locations.

We must consider this unique factor of the superintendency because it is instructive for us in terms of the types of exercises we pursue. Superintendents need some sort of daily exercise that focuses on their lower back (due to excessive periods of sitting), core exercises (to strength the posture—due to sitting), and squats (to maintain lower body strength). Each of these exercise priorities, along with the necessary aerobic workouts, can make a difference for superintendents.

Often we think about exercise in general terms based upon our past experiences or what we read, but if we can shift to considering the demands of the job we can choose exercises that will not only keep us healthy but will also prevent physical problems. Again, the superintendency is unique, and the patterns we follow on a daily basis must be considered as we develop our exercise regimen.

Reflection and Centering

The demands of the superintendency require that we find time to reflect upon complex issues and give our brains an opportunity to work through sophisticated solutions. In addition, we need time to *center* ourselves on a daily basis and possibly journal if that is helpful.

We need an opportunity to redirect ourselves toward that which keeps us going on the job and in life. In the absence of a daily centering activity we can easily find ourselves overwhelmed by the tugs and pulls of the position.

Each morning we need to go into the job focused and steady so that we are not tossed around by the issues and individuals we will face.

Often superintendents believe the best time for both reflection and centering is in the morning. We are typically fresh, and the demands of the day have yet to consume our minds, energy, and emotions. Some people pray, while others meditate. Some reflect upon their upcoming day, and others read the Bible. Regardless, it is important to purposefully set aside time for this activity. It is a form of renewal that you need mentally and emotionally.

CONCEPT 49—BRANDING YOUR DISTRICT

Social media is becoming ubiquitous, and its use as the primary tool for school district communications has arrived. Information is now available instantaneously, and districts must be nimble in keeping the public informed and dealing with negative online comments.

As this is the case, superintendents need to lead their districts in establishing an identity, or brand. If a proactive approach is not pursued, their districts will be branded for them by individuals who frequently post on social media and strategy will give way to reactive response.

Intentionally branding a school district requires the superintendent and members of the communications team (which is likely the superintendent's cabinet) to focus on a *memorable message* that they wish to promote in the minds of the public. Prior to use the message should be vetted with various members of the school community to gain feedback and ensure acceptance of the brand.

An example might be that a district brands itself *AAA*, meaning that it focuses on Academics, Arts, and Athletics. So whenever information is disseminated, the district would use messages like *Achievement Mountain Public School District—The AAA District*. The district would likely use the hashtag *#AAA* in its communications and the public would begin to associate the Achievement Mountain Public School District with the academics, arts, and athletics (or *AAA*) focus.

Another example might be that a district wants to promote the concept of its strength in all that it does (strong relationships, strong academics, strong schools, etc.). Thus, the Achievement Mountain Public School District (AMSD) might use the brand *AMSD Strong*. AMSD Strong would appear in all social media communications, but likely would also be placed on T-shirts, print communications, and so forth.

The takeaway in branding is to be sure the message is memorable and represents what the district desires to communicate about itself. In addition, the brand should be *shopped around* with district constituents prior to implementation to make sure it resonates.

Social media strategy, on the other hand, includes use of the district's brand, but more importantly looks at how to best communicate with the public and respond to criticisms. In other words, which social media sites will be used and monitored by the district? Who will make the posts and respond to both positive and negative comments? How frequently will posts appear?

Given next is a Social Media Strategy Template (exhibit 49.1). The template is designed to kick start the team's thinking as it ponders and analyzes its social media strategy.

Exhibit 49.1 Social Media Strategy Plan Template

The goal of this template is for school district teams to analyze current social media practices and to reflect upon their future strategy. As social media strategy is context specific, this template is not designed to include all possible areas of consideration, but rather should be used to initiate the analysis and planning processes.

Current Practices

Consider the following to begin the process of analyzing the school district's current status in using and responding to social media.

Questions/Comments/Process:

- Take an inventory of the current social media sites used by the district and its schools to send messages to the public, or to respond to public comments.
  - List each site and its URL.
  - Which groups tend to post on each site (parents, community, athletes, staff, etc.)?
  - List the employees (and their location) who post or respond to each site.
  - Do any sites exist that were not established by district or school employees, but that share positive or negative information?
    - Conduct a Google search for sites that list either the school district or individual school names.
    - List the URL for each site and the primary author.

Strategy Planning

Once the current practices have been identified, future strategy can be considered. In discussing future social media strategy it will be important to first identify branding messages that the district plans to use as part of the process.

Questions/Comments/Process:

- List the social media sites to be used by the district and each school.
  - Identify in the social media strategy plan the URL of each site and who will be the individual in charge initiating posts and responding to comments.
- Determine how response to negative messaging will be handled. Remember that although a quick response is important of equal importance is the quality of the response which is provided. In addition, we need to develop the wisdom to determine when a response is needed and when it is best to remain silent.
- Establish the goal in using each social media site.
  - As an example: Twitter—To provide updates and highlight achievements.
- Evaluate how the school or district brand can be woven into each message. At a minimum, include a brand hashtag.

CONCEPT 50—KNOWING WHEN TO LEAVE

Early in our superintendency we will likely hear the old joke where the outgoing superintendent provides advice to his successor. In the anecdote the outgoing superintendent indicates that if the new superintendent faces problems on the job there are three numbered envelopes in the desk drawer that can be opened and will provide deft advice.

The next spring the new superintendent receives information that district's test scores are declining and many are upset. As this is the case, the new superintendent decides to open the first envelope and inside is a card that states "blame your predecessor." Based upon this advice the new superintendent takes action to develop a statement that diplomatically places blame with the previous administration. Upon doing so the issue fades and time moves forward.

Some months later enrollment projections predict a downturn, and as a result cuts will need to be made. So, the new superintendent goes back to the drawer and opens envelope #2. Inside the card simply states to "reorganize." A reorganization process is then undertaken, and the district returns to normalcy after three months.

About two years into the position the superintendent makes the tough decision to recommend the release of a popular teacher for issues of misconduct, and an uprising takes place at the teacher's school among students, staff, and parents.

Once again, the superintendent goes back to the drawer and chooses to open envelope #3. This time the card fatefully reads "make three envelopes."

Although this was an amusing method to highlight a tough topic in the superintendency, we must realize that district leaders are in a very political role. A study conducted by the Council of Great City Schools in 2014 placed the average tenure for superintendents between three and four years. A more recent study (2018) that looked at the nation's 100 largest school districts conducted by the Broad Center placed the superintendent tenure figure closer to six years.

Regardless, the superintendency is a tough role, and although the challenges vary in different contexts, district leaders must have a sense of when to stay in a position and when to leave. It is important to note that this is a highly personal decision and will be largely dependent upon the individual's particular situation.

In other words, is the superintendent newer to the role and supporting a young family? If so, leaving a tenuous situation will likely need to be considered more quickly. Alternatively, if the superintendent already qualifies for retirement, this might change our decision-making paradigm.

Clearly there is no *right* answer in figuring out when to stay and when to leave, but there are items to consider in assessing how one might proceed if faced with a tough job situation.

- What is the history of the school district regarding superintendent turnover?
  - Unless there is a noteworthy and egregious situation the superintendent is facing, normally school boards and communities follow a pattern in terms of superintendent turnover. In other words, if the district has had five superintendents in ten years and a situation arises during the existing superintendent's tenure, it may be time for the individual to consider their options. Alternatively, if the district has typically supported long superintendent tenure in the past, it is *likely* they will continue to value stability as time progresses.
- Has the superintendent counted to three?
  - Experienced superintendents will understand this to mean that the district leader must analyze the support they enjoy with their board members. As an example, if one serves a five-member board and three board members are against the superintendent the leader will not last long in the position. Superintendents must be keenly aware during challenging situations where their support lies and how extensive it will be if a vote on their contract is required.

- How much political capital does the superintendent have in the bank?
  - This is a simple way to ask, how strong is the superintendent's relationship with his or her board and constituents? If the superintendent enjoys a strong relationship with a variety of groups ranging from parents to the teachers to business leaders, this will have an impact on how a challenging situation might play out. Although the school board will make the final decision regarding the fate of the superintendent, they will be attentive to the thoughts of their constituents. If as a whole people are supportive of the superintendent, this will have a bearing on how the board handles tough decisions related to the superintendent's tenure.
- If possible, superintendents should always leave while on top.
  - The time to leave is when things are going well for the superintendent, not when the leader is in the middle of a crisis or dealing with controversy. Following this mind-set means that superintendents must be attentive to when they search for another position and time their departure in connection with good times in the district.

This list outlines but a few of the considerations superintendents should contemplate in determining when to leave their current role. As stated earlier leaving is a highly personal decision, which involves many different individual, family, and professional considerations.

Superintendents should not be worried about the prospect of leaving their positions, but attentive to thinking through how a transition might look for them and their families if the need arises. To the extent they can have a loosely defined *exit strategy* as they enter each new role it can serve to reduce stress and prepare them for the realities of serving as a school district superintendent.

CONNECTING THE DOTS IN CHAPTER 7

This was an eclectic chapter, but it speaks to the diversity and unique nature of *living the superintendency*. On one hand, we must know ourselves and be able to assess the types of situations we are entering, but on the other, we must understand and follow the lessons of those who have gone before us in the superintendency so as to not make the same mistakes.

We must discover the discipline to live a healthy life because the demands of the job will suck us dry if allowed to do so, but we must also understand when it is time to leave. The role is rewarding, yet demanding, thus we must understand its complexities and its impact on both us and our families.

Branding our districts so that we control our identity is of growing importance. In this day and age where social media provides information on a moment's notice we must be prepared to establish and maintain our message.

Superintendents are special people who are driven to serve and must be very reflective, emotionally intelligent, knowledgeable, and self-aware to achieve success. The goal of this chapter was to cover an assortment of concepts that define this complex, challenging, yet rewarding role.

Conclusion

Accelerated Wisdom

As we conclude our journey the hope, as stated in the opening paragraphs of the book, is that you have accelerated your wisdom related to the superintendency. You may be new to the position or a veteran; regardless the desire is that you took something away from reading and reflecting upon these concepts that can make your job easier.

Most of the concepts in the book are important ideas that work. Others are meant to drive your thinking to a deeper level. None of the ideas described are purely theoretical, but rather have been tested and tried over a number of years in the superintendency.

In this day and age information is abundant and its availability is expanding at an ever-increasing pace, yet wisdom is oftentimes elusive. So rather than sifting through multiple methods to approach challenges, proven strategies were provided to assist in the daily work you do as superintendent.

Of course, each superintendent will have preferences regarding how to address a task, and each context is different, but hopefully the wisdom of experience and success provided in the book will be compelling as you continue your journey. Even if just one concept, idea, or thought makes your job easier, the benefit gained can be counted as a success.

Similar to any endeavor in which we desire success it comes down to combining hard work, stamina, knowledge, and wisdom. Hopefully you have accelerated your acquisition of wisdom through reading this book and that in some way, shape, or form are better prepared to face the challenges and complexities of the superintendency as you move forward.

In President Teddy Roosevelt's famous "Citizens in a Republic" speech he speaks to the fact that leaders enter the arena every day and toil regardless of praise or criticism. It is not always easy, but if one is mission-driven and combines enthusiasm with wisdom, great things can be accomplished. As a final thought on your role as superintendent, reflect upon and consider President Roosevelt's words provided that follow.

> It is not the critic who counts; not the man who points out how the strong man stumbles, or where the doer of deeds could have done them better. The credit belongs to the man who is actually in the arena, whose face is marred by dust and sweat and blood; who strives valiantly; who errs, who comes short again and again, because there is no effort without error and shortcoming; but who does actually strive to do the deeds; who knows great enthusiasms, the great devotions; who spends himself in a worthy cause; who at the best knows in the end the triumph of high achievement, and who at the worst, if he fails, at least fails while daring greatly, so that his place shall never be with those cold and timid souls who neither know victory nor defeat.

The words written in this speech can be an inspiration as you handle the numerous challenges that come with the role of superintendent. Although at times we may stumble and make mistakes, we also will experience great joy as we serve the students, staff, and constituents of our school district.

Always be on the lookout for the opportunity to accelerate your wisdom and to apply what you learn to this unique and wonderful role we call school superintendent. Remember, you are at the top of your career and have been placed there for a reason. Make the best of this opportunity and remember you have the power to change children's lives forever!

References

Allen, D. (2015). *Getting things done: The art of stress-free productivity.* New York, NY: Penguin Publishing.

Barsalou, M. (2015). *Root cause analysis: A step-by-step guide to using the right tool at the right time.* Boca Raton, FL: CRC Press.

Broad Center. (2018, May 8). New analysis shows the average big-district superintendent spends about six years in the job. Retrieved from https://www.broadcenter.org/about/news/new-analysis-shows-the-average-big-district-superintendent-spends-about-six-years-in-the- job/

Carlson, H. (n.d.).Three keys to a successful superintendent/school board relationship. Retrieved from http://www.aasa.org/content.aspx?id=15188

Chapman, C. (1997). *Becoming a superintendent: Challenges of school district leadership.* Upper Saddle River, NJ: Merrill Prentice Hall.

Council of Great City Schools. (Fall, 2014). Urban indicator. Retrieved from https://www.cgcs.org/

Deegan, M. (2017, July 20). Seven things you should consider before sliding into the big seat. Retrieved from https://www.linkedin.com/pulse/life-lessons-learned-through-sports-michael-deegan

Eller, J., & Carlson, H. (2009). *So now you're the superintendent!* Thousand Oaks, CA: Corwin Press.

Fullan, M. (2004). *Leading in a culture of change.* San Francisco, CA: Jossey-Bass.

Gardner, H. (2006). *Changing minds: The art and science of changing our own and other people's minds.* Boston, MA: Harvard Business School Press.

Glickman, T., Gordon, S., & Ross-Gordon, J. (2018). *Supervision and instructional leadership: A developmental approach.* New York, NY: Pearson.

Heath, C., & Heath, D. (2010, July 5). Teaching that sticks. Retrieved from https://heathbrothers.com/member-content/teaching-that-sticks/

Kotter, J. (2012). *Leading change.* Boston, MA: Harvard Business Review Press.

Kaufman, G. & Royer, R. (n.d.) *Handling Public Complaints.* Retrieved from http://convention.asbsd.org/wp-content/uploads/handling-public-complaints.pdf

Lifto, D., & Senden, J. (2010). *School finance elections: A comprehensive planning model for success*. Lanham, MD: Rowman & Littlefield Publishers, Inc.

McAdams, D. (n.d.). Getting your board out of micromanagement. Retrieved from http://www.aasa.org/schooladministratorarticle.aspx?id=4106

Meisburg, B. (2014). Balance the bridge: Enhance your communication skills and improve your life! (n.p.): Brad Meisburg.

Murphy, M. (2016). *Hiring for attitude: A revolutionary approach to recruiting and selecting people with both tremendous skills and superb attitude*. New York, NY: McGraw-Hill.

Peters., T., & Waterman, R. (2015). *In search of excellence: Lessons from America's best run companies*. London, UK: Profile Books, Ltd.

Roosevelt, T. (1910, April 23). *Citizenship in a republic* (Transcript). Retrieved from http://www.theodore-roosevelt.com/images/research/speeches/maninthearena.pdf

Watkins, M. (2003). *The first 90 days: Critical success strategies for new leaders at all levels*. Boston, MA: Harvard Business School Publishing.

About the Author

Howard C. Carlson, EdD, has been a superintendent for more than fifteen years, serving in Arizona, Minnesota, and Washington State. Dr. Carlson is coauthor of *So Now You're the Superintendent!*, a book co-published by The School Superintendents Association (AASA) and Corwin Press. He has served on the AASA Governing Board, the board of the Arizona School Administrators' Association (ASA), and the Arizona Governor's E-Learning Task Force. In 2015, he was recognized as Distinguished Administrator of the Year for the superintendent's division of ASA.

www.ingramcontent.com/pod-product-compliance
Lightning Source LLC
Chambersburg PA
CBHW030145240426
43672CB00005B/275